Praise for *Networking for People Who Hate Networking, Second Edition*

"You are going to love reading this book! Devora Zack connects with the reader like no other business author I have ever read."
—**P. J. Kuyper, President, Motion Picture Licensing Corporation**

"Devora understands the potential of the introverted networker. Her techniques will show you that what others may perceive as a weakness is actually your greatest strength."
—**Brian Tracy, author of *Eat That Frog!***

"I highly recommend this lighthearted, eminently practical book by a type-A introvert. (No, that's not a typo!) It's like having a trusted friend there at each step of the way as you become a world-class networker."
—**Jeff Martin, former Vice President, Human Resources, AOL**

"Only buy this book if you want to improve your career, connections, and social life. If that doesn't sound like you, Justin Bieber's autobiography is two shelves over."
—**Amy Lemon, Program Manager, Office of Fellowships and Internships, Smithsonian**

"No, you don't have to run around collecting business cards from every single person at every single meeting. Devora Zack proves you can make lots of new connections that help you professionally and personally while being true to who you are."
—**Jeffery Weirens, National Managing Principal, Energy, Resources, and Industrials, Deloitte Consulting, LLP**

"In the digital age, it's all too easy to ignore the real-world interactions that forge lasting relationships. We need Devora's wit and wisdom now more than ever to navigate networking in the 21st century."
—**David Meisegeier, Vice President and Senior Technical Director, ICF**

"Devora Zack returns with a much craved update to her essential networking guide. Love the new tech and new workplace context refits! Just proves everything changes except human behavior! Highly recommended!"
—**Dave Summers, Director, Digital Media Production, American Management Association**

"A tangible, practical guide to a daunting topic. Zack takes the reader by the hand and with a combination of humor and business savvy navigates effortlessly through the world of networking."
—**Howard Wiener, Principal, KPMG, LLP**

networking for people who hate networking

Who looks outside, Dreams.

Who looks inside, Awakens.

—Carl Jung

DEVORA ZACK

networking for people who hate networking

**A FIELD GUIDE
FOR INTROVERTS,
THE OVERWHELMED,
AND THE UNDERCONNECTED**

SECOND EDITION

Berrett–Koehler Publishers, Inc.

Berrett-Koehler Publishers, Inc.
1333 Broadway, Suite 1000
Oakland, CA 94612-1921
Tel: (510) 817-2277
Fax: (510) 817-2278
www.bkconnection.com

ORDERING INFORMATION
Quantity sales. Special discounts are available on quantity purchases by corporations, associations, and others. For details, contact the "Special Sales Department" at the Berrett-Koehler address above.
Individual sales. Berrett-Koehler publications are available through most bookstores. They can also be ordered directly from Berrett-Koehler: Tel: (800) 929-2929; Fax: (802) 864-7626; www.bkconnection.com.
Orders for college textbook / course adoption use. Please contact Berrett-Koehler: Tel: (800) 929-2929; Fax: (802) 864-7626.

Distributed to the U.S. trade and internationally by Penguin Random House Publisher Services.

Berrett-Koehler and the BK logo are registered trademarks of Berrett-Koehler Publishers, Inc.

Printed in the United States of America

Berrett-Koehler books are printed on long-lasting acid-free paper. When it is available, we choose paper that has been manufactured by environmentally responsible processes. These may include using trees grown in sustainable forests, incorporating recycled paper, minimizing chlorine in bleaching, or recycling the energy produced at the paper mill.

Library of Congress Cataloging-in-Publication Data

Names: Zack, Devora, author.
Title: Networking for people who hate networking : a field guide for
    introverts, the overwhelmed, and the underconnected / Devora Zack.
Description: Second Edition. | Oakland : Berrett-Koehler Publishers, [2019] |
    Revised edition of the author's Networking for people who hate networking,
    c2010. | Includes bibliographical references and index.
Identifiers: LCCN 2019000287 | ISBN 9781523098538 (paperback)
Subjects: LCSH: Business networks.
Classification: LCC HD69.S8 Z334 2019 | DDC 650.1/3--dc23
LC record available at https://lccn.loc.gov/2019000287

Second Edition
25 24 23 22 21 20 19   10 9 8 7 6 5 4 3 2 1

Designed and produced by Seventeenth Street Studios
Illustrated by Jeevan Sivasubramaniam and Jeremy Sullivan
Copyedited by Kristi Hein
Cover designed by Susan Malikowski, DesignLeaf Studio
Cover photography by Jan Will and Ben Goode, 123RF

. . . for my guys.*

*You don't expect more personal detail

than that from an introvert, do you?

contents

edition 2.0

The purpose of life is to discover your gift.
The meaning of life is to give your gift away.
—David Viscott

What a Thrill!

Hard to believe it's been nearly a decade since we first met on the mean streets of *Networking for People Who Hate Networking*, take one. We were just crazy kids with something to prove.

Plenty still holds true. We remain a hapless collection of introverts, extroverts, and centroverts. There are ample networking conundrums to navigate. Opportunities persist to trip, fall, and dust off. Lots else has changed—evolved, if you will.

The first edition sold on every continent except Antarctica. How's that for irony? I feature penguins on my book cover, and they're the ones who refrain from reading it.

Networking is now translated into fifteen languages. There are videos, ebooks, audio books, executive summaries, and whatnot. Little did I know so many would have easy access to a truckload of my most embarrassing moments.

Readers continue to share heartfelt stories about how *Networking* has changed lives, furthered careers, enabled self-acceptance, and enhanced relationships. Receiving your letters has been, by far, the best part of all.

While I've been speaking on networking, personality types, and pathways to real connections, you've provided fabulous ideas and insights on what else to integrate.

Welcome to the New and Improved Second Edition!

Beyond updates and enhancements on virtually every page, there are two additional chapters and some brand-new sections. Highlights include a chapter on follow-up, another on interpersonal networking, and a robust segment on interview tips in chapter 9, "The Job Search."

This book is not only for introverts. Even devoted extroverts donning "I ♥ Networking" T-shirts can reap benefits and learn new techniques. Extroverts will also gain insight into the mindset of introverts, making their own networking efforts yield stronger results.

With all the fancy upgrades (including our cutting-edge Get to It! Toolkit—check out the back pages for details) the book remains down-to-earth, practical, fun, and interactive. I encourage you to take part in the many activities offered throughout. I encourage you to take part in the many activities offered throughout. Since the first edition, I've written two books that can augment your networking success. *Managing for People Who Hate Managing* introduces the Thinker–Feeler (T/F) continuum, including the interplay of T/F on the Introvert–Extrovert (I/E) spectrum. *Singletasking* features methods to improve mindfulness, sharpen attention, and clarify intentions—useful skills for quality networking. The books are available in forty-five language editions.

Chapter 2 offers a self-assessment, providing the groundwork for your personalized method of networking. Content builds sequentially from there. The book is designed to be enjoyed front to back, yet you can opt to skip around, alighting on chapters with specific appeal. Plenty of options.

Notes from the Field
The Introvert Experience

Step right up! A dazzling, cutting-edge concept for a theme park ride. Patrons board an "Intromobile" and put on their introvert augmented reality (IAR) glasses. They then tour Introville while experiencing the world through the lens of an introvert. Small talk is more draining than three consecutive red-eye flights. Rallies—even for the most beloved cause—seem overblown. Privacy is at a premium.

Why wait until the permits get approved? Get started today with a low-tech alternative in the form of a handy book. Lines are under an hour with a FastPass.

this book is required reading

Only connect.

— E. M. Forster, *Howards End*

Learning Latin in Greek

On my first day of grad school at Cornell University, I attended micro-economics. The professor, in an attempt to calm our first-year jitters, explained in soothing tones that he would be showing a lot of graphs, yet there was no need to panic. He said, "Think of graphs as flow-charts, and you'll be fine." As an arts professional with no background whatsoever in economics, I suddenly felt dizzy as my vision blurred. I had never heard of a flowchart. I was doomed.

I now describe the experience of those first few weeks in business school as like trying to learn Latin in Greek . . . except I didn't know Greek either. No matter how earnestly I took notes, a few hours later I had no idea what they meant.

A comparable pitfall exists when a self-declared *non-networker* tries hard to follow networking rules written for a different species altogether. There is no point of reference. No mental bucket exists in which to dump the data. The data is fine. It is just in a foreign language. *This* networking book, on the other hand, is written in language spoken and understood by introverts, the overwhelmed, and the underconnected. What luck! You finally have a chance at a passing grade.

By the way, for many years now I have been invited back to teach networking at Cornell. I have not yet been asked to lecture on economics, however.

Networking for People Who Hate Networking

Why would such a book exist? Isn't it a bit like giving quiche recipes to people allergic to eggs and cheese? Or surrounding oneself with fragrant flowers despite suffering from severe hay fever? If you have an aversion to something not *absolutely* necessary, why not occupy your life with alternative endeavors? Why torture yourself?

These are solid questions. Thanks for asking.

Allow me to begin by saying I agree 100 percent. Do not waste a single precious hour on an activity you hate! Still, you don't get off the hook that easily. You don't get to place this book back on the shelf (or e-shelf, as the case may be), proclaiming yourself oil to networking's vinegar.

Instead, I am going to perform the astounding trick of making networking enjoyable and rewarding. All without mind-altering substances! So find a comfy chair or patch of grass, crease this spine, and commit. You won't regret it.

Our field guide begins by politely examining—and then shattering to pieces—traditional networking truisms. Commandments along the lines of:

- Promote yourself constantly.
- More contacts = higher probability of success.
- Never eat alone.
- Create nonstop touchpoints.
- Get *out there* as much as possible.

Until my first edition hit the presses, networking books were all written for people of a particular temperament—the very personality style already predisposed to relish the prospect of spearing cheese in a room full of bustling strangers.

Turns out this personality type comprises a paltry 15 percent of the general population.* I am certain this is an unintended oversight on the part of other, well-meaning authors. Nevertheless, smoke comes out of my ears just thinking about it. The other 85 percent of humankind is dismissed. Misled. Bamboozled. It is time to take back our rightful share of the networking world.

Along the way we will discover the enormous value of leveraging our natural style when networking. No more stamping out our instincts.

Why Bother?

What's that you're mumbling? You don't like networking and have no interest, anyway? It drains you? It never works? You don't have time? You don't need to? It's phony, self-serving, fake, inauthentic, superficial, conniving, manipulative, and useless?

---

*Myers, McCaulley, Quenk, and Hammer, *Myers-Briggs Type Indicator Manual* (Saint Paul, MN: Consulting Psychologist Press, 1998).

Hold it right there. Take a sip of water. Pull yourself together.

Introverts, the overwhelmed, and the underconnected fail at traditional networking by following advice never intended for us in the first place.

In my experience, people who proclaim that they hate networking also believe they are not good at it. In fact, the reverse is true. You have the raw materials to be a stellar networker. You are simply following the wrong rules. Standard networking advice fails you, so you assume you fail at networking. Plus, you *hate* it.

Finally, you can learn a method of networking in keeping with the real you. Not a moment too soon!

What's at Stake?

Only whatever you most want to accomplish in your life. No biggie.

Networking allows you to achieve your potential. Think of a Big Goal. Do you want to find a job, score a promotion, make a new contact, improve the world, expand your influence, sell a product, provide a service, write a book, seal a deal, improve collaboration, build a reputation, achieve your dream, widen your circles, or grow a business?

Networking will further your aim. In over twenty years as an executive coach, I have never met a person who did not benefit substantially from learning how to network—on his or her own terms.

What is networking, really? Networking is the art of building and maintaining mutually beneficial connections for shared positive outcomes.

Real networking is connecting.

Authenticity yields valuable, resilient networks. Ready for a networking system reliant on being true to yourself, mobilizing qualities you already have? Learn to work with, rather than fight against, your lovable introverted, overwhelmed, and/or underconnected self. Honoring your temperament is the secret to achieving your highest potential. Previously labeled liabilities are now your finest strengths.

Enticed?

Return on Investment (ROI)

Time is your most valuable asset (unless, perhaps, you are spectacularly wealthy). What about this field guide merits devoting a couple hours of your precious time to it rather than *all* the other competing options out there?

a. You will discover a super-effective, groundbreaking method of networking described in accessible, easy-to-understand language.
b. You will gain dozens of practical tips while learning clear, relevant action steps with *direct* application to your own networking goals.
c. You will benefit from myriad real-life examples spanning many fields.

Grab a pen; you'll need it. There is no such thing as a free ride. Glad to have you along.

CHAPTER 1

welcome to your field guide

Trust yourself. Then you will know how to live.

—Johann Wolfgang von Goethe

People swear up and down that I'm an extrovert.

This drives me nuts! I deny these accusations adamantly and then am subjected to a laundry list of supposed examples as to why I am mistaken. "But you're high energy! You give presentations for a living! You wrote a networking book, for crying out loud!"

Blah, blah, blah.

These people have no idea what it really means to be an introvert. They assume being an introvert *by definition* implies that one cannot be a lively, confident person or astute networker.

Together, we will dispute, disprove, and knock upside the head these assumptions.

Your Author and Tour Guide

As we embark through the uncharted terrain of networking for people who hate networking, you want to be certain you are in capable hands. Why am I qualified to lead you on this journey?

First of all, despite protests from well-intentioned, ill-advised naysayers, I am an off-the-chart introvert. I am also nearly always overwhelmed and decidedly underconnected. My idea of a good time is hanging out alone. I regularly have conversations with people in my head that I think actually took place. I need time to process ideas thoroughly before responding—or I get myself into trouble. The idea of a free-floating happy hour propels me into free-floating anxiety. A cacophony of external stimuli doesn't excite me; it drives me away. I easily and naturally pick up on nonverbal cues many others miss. I prefer a few deep relationships to a large group of friends.

As you've undoubtedly noted, none of these preferences are linked to energy level, a propensity for public speaking, or professional achievement. That's because these attributes are not related to introversion.

Let's have some fun. I will present examples of traits that, to the untrained eye, may seem extrovert-centric, but with a bit of analysis emerge as introvert-friendly.

I am Type A and move fast.

Quack "experts" profess that introverts are somehow slower paced than extroverts. This is baloney. Introverts are as likely as the next person to be highly active. Introversion ≠ lethargy! In fact, due to a penchant for heightened concentration and attentiveness, introverts are well positioned to be dynamos.

I am comfortable in front of a room.

Whoa! This combats most introvert stereotypes head on. Yet introverts are entirely capable of being public speakers. In fact, introverts prefer clearly defined roles, so many are more at ease in front of a group than roaming aimlessly through a cocktail party.

I love networking.

Herein lies the book's focus. This was not always the case for me. I discovered some wonderful techniques that turned the world of networking upside down—or shall I say right side up? You, too, can gain insights that allow you to excel at networking. You can be a networking superstar.

Seem impossible? I am here to tell you it is not.

A Brief History of the Introvert

Many readers of this book are introverts. Many have been taught through cultural cues that introversion is a problem, a deficit, something unfortunate to hide or overcome.

From a young age, introverts receive the message that it is an extrovert's world. *Go play with others. Join in on the game. Class participation is part of your grade.* Kids who withdraw around crowds are labeled as antisocial rather than applauded for being self-regulating.

Introversion is innate, and preferences are observable early on. As a kid, I asked for games to play alone—a request that could prompt some parents to conduct a thorough psychological examination. As a parent now myself, I recognized traits indicating an introverted preference in one of my sons from the age of three.

Introverts are *reflective, focused,* and *self-reliant.* These character-istics lead to the following key distinctions between introverts and extroverts:

Introverts think to talk.	**Extroverts talk to think.**
Reflective	Verbal
Introverts go deep.	**Extroverts go wide.**
Focused	Expansive
Introverts energize alone.	**Extroverts energize with others.**
Self-reliant	Social

Why not indulge yourself and utilize all three characteristics at once? Take some time to ponder these traits (*reflective*), in depth (*focused*), while alone (*self-reliant*). I'll wait here.

Regardless of temperament, linking your strengths to customized methods puts you in a primo position to network away. Introverts, extroverts, and centroverts (definition ahead!) can all benefit from this field guide.

Did I mention that I am psychic? I sense you are curious where you land in all this. Right this way . . .

CHAPTER 2

assess yourself

We do not see the world as it is. We see the world as we are.

—Anaïs Nin

Reverse It Quiz

1. Why do extroverts have voicemail?

2. Why do introverts have voicemail?

Answers:

1. To never miss a call.
2. To never answer the phone.

Identical actions can spring from divergent motivations. This point reminds us there is more to behavior than meets the eye. Some claim that observing an action is *proof* of another's motivation. This is never true. Inferences reveal only the observer's bias. The reasons *behind* behaviors reveal intentions.

Judging others? You've got it wrong.

Judging others is a misguided waste of time. Take responsibility for you. Presuming to know what's right for everyone else is a rookie mistake.

Despite his effort to get to know other executives, David may not be up for socializing every morning of the program. An opportune time for a pop quiz! What are the four most dreaded words to an introvert who has just alighted upon an empty breakfast nook, gleefully anticipating a quiet meal?

Answer: May I join you?

MENTAL ELASTICITY

Physical flexibility requires pliable muscles. Maintaining and building dexterity necessitates an ongoing commitment. Mental agility—the ability to customize responses based on circumstances—also requires continual development. This talent allows us to adapt on the fly.

Conveniently, our pals the neuroscientists (always there when needed) have a name for this phenomenon: *elasticity*. Mental elasticity can be learned and developed. This term describes the ability to be flexible in our approach to situations. Thinking in new ways builds elasticity.

From creative problem solving to crossword puzzles, anything that stretches the mind contributes to the development of a healthy, pliant mindset. Elasticity keeps brains youthful, prepared to meet challenges with fast, inspired responses.

Assessments increase elasticity by broadening your understanding of personality dimensions. Perceiving differences and identifying similarities enhances our acceptance of others. Consider this for a mantra:

> **Do not compare my insides with other people's outsides.**

Negative judgments often stem from using one's internal state to critique another's external behavior. My need to work uninterrupted may clash with your need to break up tasks with frequent, spontaneous conversations. And that's just the tip of the iceberg. People function in very different ways.

An extroverted client described herself at our initial meeting as follows: "I'm honest. I always say what's on my mind." In other words, she correlated honesty with spontaneously sharing whatever one is thinking.

"Because introverts do not have this proclivity," I queried, "does that imply they're somehow dishonest?"

She mulled this over.

At our next meeting, she announced being through with making that association. She totally got it and shifted her viewpoint. Her previous judgment that introverts are not forthcoming had been replaced by a respect for their need to process before speaking.

Try this yourself. Examine presumptions you have that may unintentionally criticize those of differing temperaments.

Spoiler alert! An elastic mindset is central to successfully "flexing your style," as featured in chapter 5.

Each number presents two statements. Assign 3 points between each pair, based on your point of view. Point distributions are 3 and 0 or 2 and 1, no half-points. If you relate to A and not to B, A = 3 and B = 0. If you agree a bit with A but more with B, A= 1 and B = 2. Respond based on your inner nature, not what you think is "right."

1.	A	Brainstorming is best when ideas are spontaneously shared.
	B	Brainstorming is best when topics are distributed in advance.
2.	A	An ideal day off features time on my own.
	B	An ideal day off is spent with others.
3.	A	People may consider me to be a private person.
	B	People may think I talk too much.
4.	A	When networking, I am good at circulating the room.
	B	When networking, I usually focus on one or two people.
5.	A	I prefer working independently.
	B	I prefer working as part of a team.
6.	A	Ideas come to me by thinking things over.
	B	Ideas come to me by talking things through.
7.	A	I prefer being with a group of people at lunch.
	B	I prefer one-on-one or alone time at lunch.
8.	A	I am uncomfortable making small talk.
	B	I am a natural conversationalist.
9.	A	I enjoy most people's company.
	B	I cherish a few true friends.
10.	A	I am often misunderstood.
	B	I am easily understood.
11.	A	I have numerous, diverse interests.
	B	I have a few interests I pursue in depth.
12.	A	Colleagues get to know me easily.
	B	Most colleagues do not know me well.

Now enter your points and total the columns.

Assessment Scorecard

1.	A = 1		B = 2
2.	B = 1		A = 2
3.	B = 0		A = 3
4.	A = 0		B = 3
5.	B = 0		A = 3
6.	B = 1		A = 2
7.	A = 0		B = 3
8.	B = 1		A = 2
9.	A = 0		B = 3
10.	B = 1		A = 2
11.	A = 2		B = 1
12.	A = 0		B = 3
Totals:	Extrovert = 7		Introvert = 29

33–36: Strong preference for your dominant style

28–32: Clear preference for your dominant style

23–27: Moderate preference for your dominant style

19–22: Slight preference for your dominant style

So, how did you do?

There are no better or worse results. It is not possible to fail!

Strength of Preference

To start with, let's clarify a few basics.

We agree there are more than two types of people. Duh! The concept of introversion and extroversion (I/E) does not imply that all extroverts—or all introverts—are precisely like everyone else in their category. Although I/E is a significant component of interpersonal style, numerous factors contribute to one's overall personality. Furthermore, *strength of preference* indicates to what degree a person identifies with defining traits for each type.

People who score 28 or higher on either scale are said to have *typed out*, to use my nerdy personality assessment lingo, as *strong* or *clear extroverts/introverts*. These people exhibit and relate to many characteristics on their side of the aisle. Those with results 23 through 27 have a moderate preference for their identifying style.

A person with a total higher score of 19 to 22 (for either column) is in the category that I dub *centroverts*. While these results indicate a very slight preference for introversion or extroversion, the distinction is so minor that this person could take the assessment again tomorrow and flip sides. A score of 18 for each, exactly in the middle, designates neither an introvert nor extrovert preference—quintessential centroverts. This happens all the time and is not cause for anxiety. Everyone has bits and pieces of both traits—it is a matter of how much one identifies with either end of the spectrum. Centroverts identify with certain traits on both sides of the spectrum.

As fate would have it, the general population is split down the middle, 50 percent closer to the introvert side and 50 percent closer to the extrovert side, with those closest to the middle now earning the extra title of centrovert.

POTENTIAL REACTIONS

Common responses to the results include:

1. This is me!
2. I'm in the middle—is that OK?
3. I knew this wouldn't work.

Let's examine and respond.

1. "This is me!" is a typical reaction when results confirm one's expectations and self-perception. Those with a strong preference along the I/E continuum often fall into this category. A higher number accompanying a dominant preference corresponds to a greater identification with descriptions of that social style.

2. "I'm in the middle—is that OK?" People with minor preferences land near the center of the I/E scale. These respondents tend to be concerned by the results, wondering, *Does this mean I am wishy-washy or somehow weak?* To the contrary. Those who score mid-range have the easiest time understanding people all along the spectrum. While the rest of us can absolutely learn to relate to different styles, this comes most naturally for centroverts, in the middle of the continuum. Other factors—such as a high self-awareness, familiarity with temperaments, or the ability to focus on others—also contribute to the ease with which one relates to different personality types.

3. "I knew this wouldn't work." At times, results contradict one's self-image, spiraling into questioning the assessment's validity. A respondent might say, "I think I'm an extrovert, but my results say I'm an introvert!" If you find yourself in this position, reflect on your mindset while responding. Were your results based on your inner nature or on how you behave in certain challenging situations? Have you taught yourself to be flexible in circumstances that demand stretching yourself? Did you possibly respond according to characteristics you covet? Do you merely have a slight affinity for I or E? Confusion can also spring from misperceptions of introversion and extroversion.

When in doubt, retake the assessment, thinking about your innate *preference*, not your learned ability or aspirations. Keep in mind your natural, internal reactions, not your dream self.

CAUTION: EXTREME READING CONDITIONS

A strong introvert displays more introverted traits than a slight introvert, and likewise for extroverts. This book highlights individuals with the clearest preference, because distinctions are most easily understood when contrasting examples at either end of the spectrum.

Ultimately, even those with identical results have differences aplenty. Innumerable factors kick in to make you unique. Everyone's journey is singular. Our aim in this field guide is to focus on one slice of personality to enhance relationship building.

A higher number accompanying your I/E preference means more examples will resonate with you. Readers with slight preferences will relate, to varying degrees, to the provided examples. The terms *strong* and *slight* reference the level of identification with one's primary style. This has no relationship to having a strong personality, firm convictions, or the ability to bench press two hundred pounds.

QUANTUM ENTANGLEMENT & INTERCONNECTIVITY

Physicists identified a phenomenon so extraordinary that Einstein nicknamed it "spooky action." It even relates to networking. Yowza!

Quantum entanglement occurs when subatomic particles interact and are then physically separated. Following the initial connection, when one of the "entangled" particles is impacted, the other instantaneously reacts—even if separated by hundreds of miles! The particles maintain a permanent connection. This is interconnectivity.

These scientific findings relate to the concept of connectivity in networking. Because people are made up of subatomic particles, entanglement has natural ramifications for human relationships. Consider colleagues who know one another superficially suddenly discovering a point of connection. Their relationship shifts permanently.

Building points of connectivity with others is a critical component of successful networking. Discovering links of commonality sharpens our receptivity to meaningful interactions.

Again and again I've seen profound results from connectivity. I frequently engage with disparate groups that at first glance may seem to have nothing in common. Other times I work with teams that have fractured relationships. Discovering and creating previously hidden links via structured, facilitated networking can be transformative. Once connectivity is established, perceptions alter, and relationships strengthen. As encounters deepen, rapport develops.

Homing in on individual relationships is a solid start. Cultivating a few meaningful connections has more tangible results than dumping a slew of cards into the ol' briefcase. Introverts are pretty darn good at connecting. Not with everyone or all the time, but our natural gravitational pull is toward lasting relationships. With the right attitude, emphasis on strengths, and a few tablespoons of willpower, you can become an expert networker—applying the personality you already have. Very handy.

I would be negligent if I didn't mention that connecting takes a tad more effort than holding up the wall, pretending to check your messages. Higher risk, higher return.

Meet me at the next chapter, where we gleefully smash to smithereens standard, shallow stereotypes.

CHAPTER 3

smashing stereotypes

Be yourself; everyone else is already taken.

—Oscar Wilde

Whaddaya Know? Quiz

True or False

1. By definition, introverts are shy.

2. By definition, extroverts are outgoing.

3. Introverts can be "fixed" by learning extroverted traits.

Answers:

1. False
2. False
3. False

Introville and Extroland

Unbeknownst to the general public, two divergent cultures live among us. Although not distinguishable by age, ethnicity, gender identity, physical abilities, or height, they are entirely different species. These two civilizations have some variations within their societies yet retain distinct customs and rituals.

Those from Introville can be identified by a propensity to vanish alone and a proclivity to make decisions while staring out a window or taking a brisk uninterrupted walk. Their depth of concentration could cause them to miss an earthquake from its very epicenter.

Those hailing from Extroland move in packs. They freely share the majority of thoughts that enter their minds, pursue new interests regularly, and make friends at every turn in the road. Even the concept of friendship has differing associations between regions, as delineated in local official dictionaries.

Due perhaps to plate tectonics, both species have been radically intermixed across the globe, even within close-knit families. There are no visible indicators of one's heritage! Litmus tests for *respect, relationships,* and *recreation* deviate. You could easily approach someone who appears to be *just like you* only to discover this person speaks a foreign language, has alien habits, and entirely misunderstands your intent.

Take heed of hasty conclusions. An introvert having a blast during a night on the town or an extrovert savoring an afternoon alone does not indicate a shift in passports or identity. Many three-dimensional beings have hidden away a sprinkling of their own opposites blended in for flavor.

To make this dynamic even more colorful, please join me in welcoming the centroverts to our region. Centroverts are a sizable community originating from the border between Introville and Extroland—simultaneously at home in both and neither of the two nations.

Your sole hope to manage this complex demographic phenomenon? A quality field guide. At your service.

STEREOTYPING THE DAY AWAY

What traits and associations do the terms introvert and extrovert bring to mind? Glad you asked. Thank your lucky stars, as I've queried thousands on that precise topic and compiled the predominant responses for your exclusive perusal:

Common (Specious!) Introvert Stereotypes

Aloof	Antisocial	Awkward	Boring
Cagey	Detached	Distant	Elusive
Insecure	Isolated	Low-energy	Moody
Negative	Nerdy	Private	Quiet
Reclusive	Rude	Secretive	Shy
Slow	Snobby	Spacey	Standoffish
Testy	Troubled	Unfriendly	Uninteresting

Common (Irresponsible!) Extrovert Stereotypes

Annoying	Attention-grabbing	Brash	Cliquey
Clueless	Draining	Egocentric	Fake
Inappropriate	Insensitive	Intrusive	In your face
Loudmouth	Manipulative	Noisy	Nosey
Poor listener	Pushy	Relentless	Schmoozer
Self-engrossed	Self-promoter	Shallow	Shameless
Show-off	Superficial	Talkative	Too much information (TMI)

It doesn't take a rocket scientist to recognize that most of these descriptors have negative connotations. Nevertheless, any and all rocket scientists are welcome to weigh in.

These lists provide examples of perceptions based on misnomers and assumptions. None are empirically true. As in "two is greater than one" true. We get this intellectually. We do not, however, always function from our intellect. To quote the charming band the Lemonheads, "Slipped my mind that I could use my brain."* Well put.

It turns out labels such as *shy* and *outgoing* have no direct correlation with introversion and extroversion. There are outgoing introverts (right here!) and extroverts who identify with shyness. Introverts can be friendly, and extroverts can be reflective. Extroverts, centroverts, *and* introverts all have natural strengths. No one wins by attempting to emulate other personality types.

Now that we've cleared up the basics, I am compelled to make a proclamation:

Introverts do not need to be fixed!

Everybody is more than fine as they are. When we tap rather than cap our true nature, the sky is the limit.

A Crash Course in Introverts

Repeat after me: "Introversion is not pathology!" Or write it down. No need to speak, interrupting your train of thought.

Remember the Big Three characteristics in chapter 1? They're back and better than ever, providing the foundation of Introville residents' distinguishing traits.

---

*The Lemonheads, "It's a Shame About Ray," *Rudderless* (Atlantic Records, 1992).

Introversion is about what goes on internally, not what

is observed externally.

The introvert's inner motivation is hidden to all but the most gifted observer.

Notes from the Field
Introvert Spotting

How do you spot the elusive, chameleon-like introvert? With difficulty. Overall, introverts seem to be better equipped to sight an extrovert than vice versa. I rarely encounter an introvert who is surprised to learn that a stranger who spontaneously related his life story is a citizen of Extroland.

It can be more difficult to determine with certainty that one is in the company of an Introville native. Here are observations, supplied by actual introverts, about their compatriots' revealing habits!

- She evaporates with no forwarding address, emerging refreshed.
- He takes a lot of notes, referencing them prior to speaking up.
- She sits at the far corner table during business trip breakfasts.
- He opts out of optional evening programs and events.
- Even after significant shared time, she refrains from sharing basic facts about herself.
- He takes his time with opinions yet has firm convictions.

Once, a seminar participant asked me whether personality style impacts the way colleagues greet one another at work, prompting me to ask the group how they acknowledge others when passing in the hallway. A strong introvert replied, "I raise my eyebrows." We busted up laughing. How quintessential.

Happy exploring! On your journey, bring patience, silence, your phone in camera mode, and an acute sense of humor. Introverts pop out of hiding when you least expect it.

Introverts Think to Talk (Reflective)

Introverts process the world by thinking through and reflecting upon our initial impressions and perceptions. Therefore, we require a bit of time to properly respond to new data and requests. Introverts *can* reply without thinking—but these reactions are likely to be inaccurate or incomplete.

An introvert can become quite chatty when bonding with another person—whether that person is an introvert, extrovert, or centrovert. Just as likeminded people are drawn together, opposites also attract. Think about a time you clicked with someone. Did you surprise yourself with how talkative you became? Introverts aren't necessarily quiet. Our talk-o-meter rating is quite circumstantial.

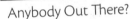

Notes from the Field
Anybody Out There?

I was on the phone with a new client. We had not met face-to-face. I asked a question, and he paused so long I thought we had been disconnected. Loath to interrupt his process, I waited and waited. Eventually I asked awkwardly, "Hello? Are you still there?"

"Yes." He struggled to explain: "My mind works faster than my words."

Ding! Ding! An introvert clue, I thought to myself. A couple of weeks later, I told him of my internal response to his internal processing, and we laughed at this example of introverts in conversation.

Introverts Go Deep (Focused)

Introverts can get absorbed in a task, losing ourselves in the moment. We pursue interests in depth and are selective in relationships. Introverted networking emphasizes deeper interactions with fewer individuals—a practice with high potential for lasting relationships.

Introverts don't do well with interruptions. It is jolting to be unceremoniously pulled away from a project. Here's a play-by-play. Concentrating on a task, you *become* the task. You enter the flow of the cosmos. An extrovert whizzes by, cheerfully asking whether you want to join a group heading out for, well, anything. You decline. Then you can't quite pick up where you left off. It's over. Bye-bye, flow.

Breaking news! When an extrovert pops her head into an introvert's cubicle to say, "Hey! How ya doing?" What the introvert really wants to respond is, "Fine, until you asked how I was doing."

Introverts Energize Alone (Self-Reliant)

Introverts are inner-directed. This means we reenergize by being alone. Introverts crave individual time (I-time) as if it were oxygen in the lungs for survival. Inadequate I-time can result in exhaustion, imbalance, shortness of breath, and irritability. Reserves run dry. Alone time is nonnegotiable for a high-functioning introvert. Honoring, rather than ignoring, this need allows introverts to direct their attention to social demands such as networking, with exceptional results.

Three corollaries. First, being with a close friend or family member can also energize. Second, it is perfectly natural for introverts to consider coexisting in a shared space, while doing their own thing, as quality time. Third, when socializing we typically prefer one-on-one to group gatherings.

- Strong sense of subtle observation   →   - Attuned to nonverbal indicators

- Innately independent   →   - Think for themselves

- Attention on internal   →   - Do not notice or care much about externalities

A FEW HAZARDS OF INTROVERSION

- Heightened need for privacy   →   - Extroverts can experience relationships with introverts as uneven or one-way

- Difficulty handling interruptions   →   - Networking requires adapting to mercurial conversations

- Drained by small talk   →   - Simple banter can wipe out an introvert's energy

A Crash Course in Extroverts

At first glance, extroverts seem to be naturally adept networkers. When I teach courses on *Networking for Extroverts and Introverts*, the introverts respond with shock that any extrovert would ever voluntarily attend such a seminar. Don't the extroverts have it all wrapped up?

Yet voluntary enrollment hovers at fifty-fifty.

It turns out the extroverts have plenty to learn—from introverts!—about networking. What a shocker. Once we pass around the smelling salts to revive those with a fainting proclivity, we proceed. In these seminars, stereotypes are crushed. It turns out even extroverts have networking challenges.

Plenty of people you meet and network with are extroverts. So pull yourself together, put on your field gear, pick up your tablet, and (if you're not an extrovert yourself) set out to understand this mysterious culture.

There is no better or worse. Deeper understanding results in greater appreciation of others' offerings. Ready for our trek into extrovert territory?

An introvert's cacophony is an extrovert's symphony.

Welcome to Extroland!

Notes from the Field
Teamwork

Sometimes I separate out introverts and extroverts before assigning tasks. The introverts start by asking, "Do we need to do this as a team?" I say yes.

Meanwhile, the extroverts are rapidly bonding. They shout out over each other. No one cares. They don't check in with each other regarding agreement to responses. No one is offended; they're engaged and excited. They quickly volunteer to share their results, proclaiming, "We'll go!"

When an introvert volunteers, she begins by checking in with the group to ensure that no one minds if she shares their discussion points. Her raised hand is not accompanied by calling out. Each contribution is explained, and she withholds any information deemed personal.

These composite examples draw on hundreds of programs in which I have seen astonishingly consistent results.

While we hover near the topic, I want to dispel once and for all the misnomer that introverts are not good team players. It is time to put this unseemly rumor to rest. Naïve people (gift them this book) subscribe to the faulty logic that because introverts are inner-directed they do not play well with others. Introverts can be exemplary contributors, with an attention to detail, creative approach, and uncanny ability to see beyond the surface.

I will concede one point. When on a team, an introvert prefers a discrete task and the autonomy to carry it out.

Extroverts Talk to Think (Verbal)

Extroverts process verbally—clarifying what they think through discussion. Herein lies a distinction between these two adjoining terrains. Let me be clear—extroverts *talk* to *think*. This is so fundamentally disparate from the introvert's core that it leads to an abundance of differences.

Speaking enables extroverts to work through ideas. Therefore, extroverts may express opinions they discount moments later. Extroverts are not necessarily committed to their spoken ideas, as speaking aloud enables them to discover what they *truly* think.

This is a major departure from what goes on in Introville where words are carefully weighed before utterance. You can imagine this is a source of much angst between the territories.

Extroverts Go Wide (Expansive)

Whereas introverts delve deeply into projects and relationships, extroverts gravitate to an assortment of experiences. Extroverts cast a wide net on a plethora of topics.

Extroverts are likely to exhibit a sincere interest in many arenas—however briefly. Extroverts enjoy environments that merge stimuli, activities, and options. More is more.

These tendencies serve them well in networking circles when meeting a mix of people.

In Extroland, variety is the spice of life.

Extroverts Energize with Others (Social)

Extroverts gain energy from socializing. That's right, extroverts are *energized* by conversing. For the garden-variety introvert, drained by small talk, this is a difficult concept to grasp. Yet some introverts will grudgingly admit that they envy extroverts this trait.

Extroverts in my seminars have been known to proclaim, "I can talk to anyone about anything!" Introverts stare, stunned, as if upon a UFO sighting.

SAMPLE BENEFITS OF EXTROVERSION

- Spontaneous interactions → Engage in conversation effortlessly
- Comfort in unfamiliar situations → At ease in diverse situations
- Release of grudges or slights → Take few things personally

A FEW HAZARDS OF EXTROVERSION

- Poor follow-up → Prefer in-the-moment to closing-the-loop
- Provide a surfeit of information → Can ramble or provide unnecessary details
- Freely share private informations → A lower bar for what is deemed personal*

Are You *Really* Underconnected?

Online platforms such as LinkedIn, Facebook, and Twitter carry distinct associations for introverts and extroverts. Extroverts are excited by the prospect of expanding networks to unprecedented size and scope. Daily updates come naturally. For introverts, keeping active online can present as a necessary nuisance, weighing down their to-do list.

The term *super-connector* typically refers to someone who has an extraordinary number of connections. Extroverts are more likely to

---

* An extrovert reviewed this summary of hazards and protested, "What's wrong with openly sharing private information? Why is that a hazard?" In the spirit of free speech, her opinion must be heard. Contemplate both sides of the issue.

acquire this label, due to their typically wider circles of business associates and online connections.

Because introverts value depth—usually manifesting as fewer, stronger connections—it is not possible for an introvert to reference hundreds of people as friends. That is a carefully guarded term for the select few. Relationship maintenance is more demanding for introverts, who nurture relationships with customized interactions.

Will the real *super-connector* please stand up? Is it the person with loads of electronic friends, effortlessly updated with a click of the Send button, or the one with fewer connections, invested in years of developing affinity and trust?

Social scientists profess it is not possible to maintain hundreds, let alone thousands, of friends. A widely held standard, Dunbar's number, caps our capacity for social networks at 150 individuals.

Let's deconstruct the term *super-connector*. Does *super* necessarily imply high volume? Or can it mean doing something exceptionally well? As time is finite, greater quantity inevitably correlates with decreased depth of connection.

> *Super [as prefix]*: over and above; higher in quantity, quality, or degree.
>
> *Connect*: 1. to become joined. 2. to have or establish a rapport.
>
> —*Oxford English Dictionary*

The prefix *super* can reference higher quantity *or* quality. The verb *connect* can mean simply joining (as in a club, association, or community) *or* establishing lasting rapport. Does breadth or depth of connections merit the prefix *super*? There is no right answer. Your response depends on perspective and preferences.

Therefore, whether you label yourself or others as underconnected depends on your definitions. Going for quality and rapport is not so shabby. You have my permission to replace the prefix *under* with *super* for a small, albeit devoted, network.

CHAPTER 4

why we hate to network

Be kind. For everyone you know is fighting a great battle.

—Philo of Alexandria

Grrrr . . . Quiz

1. Why *do* you hate networking?

   a. It is a waste of time, without value.

   b. It's in your blood.

   c. You are incapable, and that's that.

Answer:

   b. Literally! And in your genes. Read on . . .

Saber-Toothed Tigers and You

Entering a networking event, a half-hour after kickoff, you're bombarded with sounds and activity from all sides. Your heart rate increases, your pulse speeds up, and adrenaline races through your veins. (Is that all the same thing? You get the idea.) Imperceptible beads of perspiration form.

You involuntarily glance at your watch, although you arrived a moment before. Why did you come to this event? You must have had a logical reason, but it is fading fast. You hate this stuff and aren't in the mood for a bunch of superficial baloney. To think that instead of being here you could be relaxing alone—even reading a networking book would be preferable. Now that's a low bar!

You vaguely recall a stress-management seminar in college. The instructor said to breathe deeply when under stress. What annoying advice! If he were here right now you'd tell him what you thought of his ridiculous breathing.

Hold it right there.

Let's take a trip down memory lane—way before your college shenanigans. To the days of the saber-toothed tigers and early humans. Our environment has changed enormously since then, but human physiology hasn't altered all that much. In earlier times, when a person perceived himself to be in danger, he likely was in a life-threatening situation. The physical response was to jolt into the *fight-or-flight* state. His body prepared to either run like crazy and get the heck out of there or fight like his life depended on it—which it probably did.

We humans are stuck in the past.

Fast-forward to the networking program you just entered. Your mind identifies the event as threatening, and your body reacts as if a saber-toothed tiger might leap through the wall at any moment. Although today this is rarely the case, our physiological responses still kick in with the fight-or-flight response.

Most of your blood flows to your extremities to prepare for battle or a speedy run. Where does all that extra blood come from? Great question! Your brain donates blood to your arms and legs. This exodus of blood from your head leaves you unable to think clearly. When someone approaches you with a friendly greeting, your response is muddled; you are a shadow of your potentially vivacious self.

I hate to tell you this, but the old adage about taking a few deep breaths is valid. When stress causes our physiology to direct blood to the extremities, breathing gets shallow, not entirely filling the lungs. Sometimes we even hold our breath without realizing it. As the brain's blood flow depletes, rational thought takes a nosedive.

Drawing oxygen down to the diaphragm (below the rib cage) improves circulation. Deep breathing triggers a relaxation response. Panic subsides, normal blood flow is restored, and thoughts clarify. Before presentations I find a quiet spot. At times a bathroom stall is as swanky as it gets. A few deep breaths clarify thoughts and increase receptivity. It works, it's fast, it's portable, and it's free. It doesn't get much better than that.

I was speaking at a Mensa International conference. To give you a flavor of the event, the speaker following my keynote pontificated on "String Theory for Everyone." A heady program, to be certain.

As attendees were spread across several hotels, on the first morning I boarded a shuttle bus to get to the conference center. I attempted to blend unnoticed into the back row of seats. I failed instantly, having forgotten about my nametag proclaiming "Presenter" in large block letters. A revved-up extrovert plopped down next to me, inquiring about my speaking topic. "Networking techniques," I squeaked out, unconvincingly. She looked skeptical.

Once inside the mazelike headquarters, I sought out a remote corner of a café to sit alone and sip a latte prior to my presentation. Fate intervened. The same perky extrovert appeared, standing over my table, laughing, "So, *this* is how you kickoff networking?!" She gestured at the empty space surrounding me.

I nodded with conviction. "Yes, exactly like this."

What others may see: An isolated introvert, missing opportunities.

What's occurring: A person with a plan, gathering energy reserves for optimal results.

Searching for a Palm Tree

So you consider yourself overwhelmed or underconnected. You'd prefer scheduling a root canal over schmoozing with a group of strangers. Perchance you blame yourself. Hold it.

The reality is, ordinary networking advice fails most introverts, centroverts, and even many extroverts. We erroneously declare, "If *that* is how to network successfully, then I am a networking train wreck." As if old-fashioned tips such as "more is more" are indisputable guidelines, and there's nothing we mortals can do about it. Upon closer examination, the reality is different indeed.

Follow me on this one.

Let's say I lived in Miami and wrote a guidebook on how to locate palm trees. "Go outside, walk around a while, look up, and you'll spot one soon enough," I would write, reasonable advice for a Floridian. But what if an aspiring palm tree searcher in Boise, Idaho, purchased my guide? He would earnestly attempt to follow my guidelines, walk around for hours, and return home in despair. His conclusion? He hates searching for palm trees and is terrible at it. Demoralized, he vows to avoid this activity at all costs in the future. He blames himself, interpreting the disconnect as his own shortcoming. Eventually he may realize the book simply wasn't written for him in the first place.

Like the palm tree book, other networking advice isn't inherently flawed; it's merely geared to a subgroup of the population. The rest of us are left out in the cold, wandering aimlessly.

Saying "I'm a bad networker" becomes the equivalent of "I am a bad extrovert." That makes about as much sense as "I am bad at writing with my right hand" when I am left-handed. Why don't I instead focus on being a gifted left-hander? Why refute my natural style?

Want a different approach? Me too! First, accept who you are. Then work with your strengths. Buck the system!

CATASTROPHIC THINKING

Catastrophic thinking is one of my favorite cognitive distortions, and a modern twist on the saber-tooth threat. An event occurs. Rather than thinking, *That event occurred!* you instead embark on an exhilarating journey to catastrophic thinking. In a nutshell, your psyche transforms temporary setbacks into full-scale disasters, leaving you in a disheveled heap.

Reframing

Whether you love, tolerate, or hate networking is directly correlated to your inner monologue. It is never too late to rewire your brain! All you need is a small set of pliers and a dose of willpower.

Moving forward, I will reference the term *reframing*. Like many beloved concepts, it is both unassuming and widely applicable. Imagine you own a painting in an ordinary metal frame. One day you reframe it, selecting a riveting customized frame, accentuating the picture's colors. The artwork itself appears transformed. That's how reframing works.

We frame experiences based on our perceptions and our past. Testing out a new cognitive framework can dramatically shift our experience of events and people. Altering perceptions enables a change in response and behavior. Reframing is a handy concept for overwhelmed, underconnected non-networkers.

Do you think you're a lousy networker? Why? Many people associate networking with working a room: approaching strangers, making chitchat, and freely divulging personal information. What if we reframe networking as an opportunity to create meaningful connections, requiring thoughtfulness and sensitivity? Do you think you have these abilities? Does this change your visceral response to the concept of networking?

A centrovert coworker whom I've known for years lights up when engaged in conversation and seeks out opportunities to mingle. Yet she shies away from promoting her services, despite expertise and impeccable credentials. She recently shared why: "I don't like asking for things."

I asked, "Wait, what? Don't you believe in what you offer?"

She learned to replace the idea of *needing* with that of *providing*. Reframing enabled her to redefine networking as an opportunity for collaboration. She focuses on ways to increase others' success, rather than asking for favors.

I was coaching a vice president of an international development company. His direct reports and close colleagues produced a string of superlatives to describe his style—to such an extent that I could gather infuriatingly few areas for development. However, his career seemed to have stalled out at its present level, and we explored why this was the case. He revealed that he was not good at promoting his accomplishments. He felt inadequate in the realm of organizational politics, and he suspected—correctly— that those in the highest leadership roles were unaware of his strengths and successes.

He was continually passed over for promotion opportunities. He identified as an introvert, with most of the defining, correlating qualities. Despite widespread respect from trusted coworkers, he needed to convey his value to those in more senior positions. As his global company offered few opportunities for face-to-face meetings, he began sending biannual progress reports to the leadership team, always keeping the bulleted list to under a page.

At the next annual meeting, he was determined to introduce himself to those on his short distribution list. He made personal contact, kept current on company achievements, followed up with thank-you notes, and inquired occasionally about new opportunities on the horizon. He was promoted a year later.

You have much to offer. Let that conviction permeate your networking opportunities.

Self-Talk

Do you mentally beat yourself up, retaining beliefs that you aren't interesting, worthy, or confident? What audio loop runs through your daily consciousness?

Self-talk is how we speak to ourselves within our heads. Themes emerge. Some patterns place a negative veneer on events; others emphasize the positive. Here is a summary of these styles.

Negative Self-Talk	Positive Self-Talk
▪ Catastrophic	▪ Manageable
▪ Discouraging	▪ Encouraging
▪ Emotive	▪ Reflective
▪ Exaggerated	▪ Realistic
▪ Grim outlook	▪ Good humor
▪ Limiting	▪ Expansive
▪ Victim	▪ Learner

Let's dispel the myth that negative self-talk is somehow more honest. To the contrary, negative self-talk tends to exaggerate the impact of what occurred:

It was a disaster! I blew it and will never recover.

Positive self-talk tends toward specificity:

I am looking to make a career change and went to an industry event. It's true: I dripped artichoke dip down the front of my white shirt shortly after walking in. At one point I accidentally introduced myself using the other person's name because I was looking at his name tag and was distracted. But I crossed the hurdle of getting out there, and everyone messes up sometimes. I'll make up for it with strong follow-up.

Negative self-talk attributes blame. Positive self-talk takes responsibility, replacing a victim's perspective with a learner's approach.

How could this happen? → What can I learn?

Try this technique.

Take Action!
"Self-Image and Networking"

Recall a time you engaged in negative self-talk. Write the sequence of events in the left-hand column. In the middle column, list your negative thoughts during and after the experience.

Now imagine alternative, supportive responses. Write these in the right-hand column. What could be the effect of shifting your inner reactions? If you have a pal nearby, this can be a shared activity. Complete your first and second columns, then swap forms and each of you review what the other wrote. Fill out each other's "revised" column, trade back, and discuss.

Event(s)	My Perceptions and Negative Self-Talk	Revised, Supportive Self-Talk

Here is a sample completed form, a riff from our "Botched Networking with Artichoke Dip" example.

Event(s)	My Perceptions and Negative Self-Talk	Revised, Supportive Self-Talk
Hoping for a career change, I signed up for a networking event with influential people. I was late and hungry. I came straight from work and promptly dripped artichoke dip down my shirt front. Then I introduced myself to an industry leader using *his* name. I took his card to end the conversation and left soon after.	They have to schedule construction during rush hour, making me half an hour late to this darn event that I shelled out forty bucks to attend. I was famished. Like a complete idiot, I start shoveling in this green dip to take the edge off my hunger, and wouldn't you know it? Spill it all over my white shirt. Embarrassed and distracted, I am approached by this bigwig sticking his hand out; I look at his nametag and I introduce myself as him. This guy couldn't believe how stupid I am; I could see it in his eyes. When I asked for his card, he probably wished he didn't have one.	I am proud of myself for taking a concrete step toward a career change. I hit traffic, learning a lesson to leave earlier. I spilled dip on my shirt but got most of it off with a napkin. The rest was hardly visible behind my tie. Next time I'll take the edge off my hunger before arriving. It was great that the guy who arranged the event made a point of introducing himself to me, and we got a laugh out of my faux pas when I said his name for my own. I can make a humorous reference to it when I thank him in a note tomorrow.

It is harder to wash away unwanted habits than to scrape price tag residue off newly purchased glassware. Negative self-talk is sticky. Tips are in order.

1. Negative self-talk is widespread and reversible. Resist the urge to have negative self-talk about your negative self-talk, if you catch my drift.

2. Rather than attempting to cease all limiting thoughts, initially commit to merely increasing your awareness. Making self-talk conscious is a first step.

3. While the brain can *do* something, it can't *not do* something. Ask a cognitive scientist—there must be one around here. It is futile to think *I shouldn't think those thoughts.* You've probably heard the "Don't envision a pink elephant" illustration; if not, never mind. When you have negative self-talk, practice following it up with a revised, positive version.

It is worth the effort. Improving self-talk requires little investment, as it is contained in that gorgeous head of yours. Positive self-talk improves perspective, attitude, and mood. All this combines to convey a more confident self-image.

Additional Networking Misdemeanors

Manners in a digital world are a whole new ballgame. Modern communication can backfire regardless of best intentions. Digital age interactions bring hazards. Abiding by certain guidelines can help circumvent networking disasters.

1. Never forward an email or text without the originator's explicit approval. I've seen careers derail from this oversight, more than once.
2. Only "Reply All" if explicitly requested. No one wants to get lost in a torrent of Reply All's.
3. Don't release into the cosmos *any* message you'd regret being viewed by an unintended recipient.
4. Review significant messages before sending. Let a trusted source provide feedback and edits on important messages before sending.
5. Never hit Send when you're still seeing red. Or when not fully conscious. There are apps to delay outgoing messages to prevent sender's remorse. Once it's released, it's show time.
6. Any time a call is on speakerphone and others are within earshot, begin the conversation by mentioning that fact. Extroverts may need to be reminded.
7. Written messages have no intonation and are super easily misconstrued, particularly on sensitive topics. Plus, rushing backfires all too often, and you know it.

Know when and how to wrap up a digital conversation. Don't be a party to endless exchanges. Offer natural conclusions to message chains:

- I'll see you there.
- I'll send a calendar invite.
- Unless I hear otherwise, we're on.
- No reply necessary.

Be gracious on the receiving end. If you receive a document, shoot off, "Thanks, I got it!" or "We appreciate your time." Human nature inventively fills in for a lack of communication. I was asked to edit an article with a tight deadline. After significant effort, I was never privy to a response or acknowledgment. My brain determined that my input was construed as useless, offensive, or at best taken for granted.

A smidgen of analog advice for extroverts. Verbalizing whatever's on your mind feels natural. This carries benefits and potential hazards. A beloved instructor in a class I attended was fired for joking with a new student who was unaccustomed to her tongue-in-cheek style. In another scenario, a consultant who prided himself on relationship building spent so much time chatting about nonwork-related updates that the client got exasperated and ended the contract.

Awareness of potential pitfalls helps maintain viable connections.

CHAPTER 5

good-bye, golden rule

My idea of an agreeable person is a person who agrees with me.

—Benjamin Disraeli

Making the Most of It Quiz

Why do introverts tend toward perfectionism?

Answer:

Combining an inner focus with a susceptibility for
deep pondering leads to a propensity for perfection.

The Platinum Rule

The golden rule is one of the most quoted edicts in the parlance of being nice to other people. There may be as many versions of the golden rule as there are languages. It can be paraphrased succinctly:

◇◇◇◇ **GOLDEN RULE** ◇◇◇◇

Treat others as you want to be treated.

Why not? Seems logical. Although what really happens when following the golden rule to the letter?

An introvert and an extrovert are colleagues in the same department. They attend a networking event together. Each believes firmly in the golden rule.

Upon arrival, Glen the extrovert gleefully descends on a group already gathered in the center of the room. He joins in, pulling Portia the introvert along with him. He knows she can recede in a crowd. He likes Portia and wants her to have a good time. The conversation turns to presentation mishaps, and he recalls Portia's fiasco the day before. "Hey Portia! Tell them about your hilarious faux pas yesterday!" He means well and knows the event had no lasting or important consequence. Meanwhile, Portia is inwardly mortified. The last thing she wants to do is recount an embarrassing personal story to a group of complete strangers.

Now let's take the opposite path. Same setup, Portia and Glen at the event. Portia, as an introvert, is super-sensitive about what is potentially personal while networking. She is asked by a small cluster of newly met acquaintances about a recent success she enjoyed at work. Although she knows Glen also had a similar experience, she hesitates to bring it up in case Glen considers that to be a private piece of information. Glen feels dissed that Portia didn't create the obvious natural bridge from her story to his own.

Both scenarios exemplify the golden rule: the colleagues are treating one another as they themselves would like to be treated. The result? Each is unhappy with the outcome.

Instead, I propose the new and improved (cue fanfare):

◇◇◇◇ **PLATINUM RULE** ◇◇◇◇

Treat others how they want to be treated!

The scintillating Platinum Rule revolutionizes interactions and relationships, particularly among introverts, centroverts, and extroverts. That would be, um, everyone.

The Platinum Rule is certainly more work than the golden rule. If I use the golden rule, I get to act the same way all the time. It's easy. I consider the treatment that I like and treat everyone that way. Unfortunately, due to diverse preferences and perceptions, I will be less than fully effective most of the time. To apply the Platinum Rule, two challenging skills come into play:

1. I can, with some success, assess others' natural proclivities.
2. I am capable of modifying my interactive style to strengthen relationships.

One size does not fit all. Different folks, different strokes. Expecting that others will adjust to our style is not realistic. Most people lack the skills or awareness to artfully apply the Platinum Rule. That is why it is up to us. Do not despair! No one has to get it right completely or all the time. Even with imperfection, the benefits are boundless. Rapport soars and networks blossom. The effort pays off.

Before understanding the divide between Introville and Extroland, it's tempting to react with annoyance over behaviors incongruent with one's own sensibilities. Yet now, affinity gleefully overcomes frustration. Judgment is replaced with humor, irritation with gratitude.

BE A SLEUTH

Reframe yourself as a detective, always on the lookout for clues. People bombard us with cues about how their minds work, how they function, and how they like to be treated. Tuning in to these verbal and nonverbal hints enables us to calibrate our communication, upping the likelihood of a positive response. You can practice fine-tuning your ability to pick up on nonverbal cues anywhere you go. A side benefit is that you never again have to be bored at a meeting or while waiting in line. Soak it all in.

Notes from the Field
A World Apart

Two young men approached me during an executive development seminar to discuss a "difficult, negative" colleague. Describing Anne, they shook their heads in baffled exasperation. Their description of her incorrigible behavior culminated with this anecdote: "We have a birthday club, so we can all celebrate together. She refuses to even tell us her birth date!"

They paused for air, clearly expecting me to jump on the bandwagon. Instead, a realization hit me. "Wait a minute. Is this the Anne in our class?" Yes, they confirmed.

I recognized Anne as a strong introvert. Among other behaviors: she listened intently, alternating with mentally removing herself for internal processing. In the course of our two days together I had observed Anne as quick-witted, delightfully sincere, and notably supportive of teammates.

These two well-intentioned extroverts could not fathom why someone would rebuff an effort to join in on friendly group celebrations. Her refusal was jolting, interpreted as difficult behavior. They had stopped speaking to her altogether. Yet where Anne comes from, one's birthday is personal. The prospect of regular group celebrations at work seemed tedious and superficial. The same birthday celebrations that invigorated the extroverts were uncomfortable and draining to Anne.

I explained how people interpret events and exchanges differently. I recommended they neither ostracize Anne nor expect her to conform to their definition of having fun. We discussed ways to rebuild a collegial professional relationship. Starting with a smile and nod as they passed her desk, and slowly growing from there.

The follow-up status reports I received were heartening.

While facilitating programs, I notice how frequently the concept of respect comes into the group discussions. Participants implore:

- We need to respect each other more!
- She doesn't respect me.
- No one respects each other around here.
- It is obvious he isn't respectful to others.

What is going on? Are humans hopelessly disrespectful? Nope. The problem is more easily solved than that.

Respect is a vague concept that defies measurement. It is not easily defined. People are multidimensional, and respect is experienced subjectively.

Let's say Marge, an introvert, is out on personal leave for two weeks. One of her extroverted coworkers, Marissa, wishes to express respect for her acquaintance. She employs the golden rule, treating Marge as she herself would want to be treated. When Marge returns to the workplace, Marissa dashes over affectionately, pats Marge on the arm, and says loudly, "Hey Margie! Glad you are back! Is everything okay? If you need to talk about anything, my door is always open."

How do you surmise Marge is responding internally? Most likely she is feeling invaded. She does not know Marissa well. She thinks it is inappropriate for Marissa to be so chummy, and she is uncomfortable with being touched by a virtual stranger. Plus, she does not appreciate Marissa's making a scene in front of everyone.

Now an opposite scenario. Guapo, an extrovert, has also been away for two weeks on personal leave. His introverted colleague, Josh, sees Guapo return to work on Monday morning. Wanting to be respectful, Josh treats Guapo the way he himself would want to be treated. He politely says hello, behaving as if nothing unusual has happened. Why draw attention to someone who has clearly been dealing with some personal issue?

Guapo is hurt. He thinks, *How rude and insensitive of Josh! We have worked together for six months, I am out of the office on personal leave, and Josh acts as if I was here yesterday. Obviously, he doesn't care about anything but my productivity.*

Do you see the issue? In each case, the well-intentioned colleagues, Marissa and Josh, are employing the golden rule, treating a coworker as they themselves would want to be treated. In both cases, their efforts backfire entirely. Seeing the results of their earnest efforts, Marge and Guapo are taken aback and even offended. Each would report being disrespected.

How does the Platinum Rule reverse this? First, Marissa and Josh would be self-aware enough to understand their own interactive styles. They would also be astute observers of coworkers' behaviors, gaining insight into how they might want to be treated. They fall short at times but make an effort. Finally, they develop the skill to modify their communication styles, calibrating their responses. This is a great place to apply the concept of mental elasticity, introduced in chapter 2.

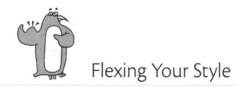 Flexing Your Style

It is a fine line. On the one hand, I say be true to who you are. On the other, I say it is an important networking talent to know how to flex your style, known in the world of personality assessment as *engaging out of type*. How do we reconcile this apparent contradiction? The answer goes back to the inside and the outside.

Your internal drivers remain largely consistent. You are who you are. Yet conscious choices can mold behavior. The more you heighten your observational powers and practice flexing your style, the more choices are at your disposal.

The sophistication to draw upon a range of behaviors based on circumstance increases one's probability of forming real connections with all personality types. I have delightful, lifelong relationships with flaming extroverts. And the reason I am frequently labeled as an extrovert myself is that I can flex my own external style—and even enjoy it! It's what goes on behind the scenes, as I recharge, that belies a casual observer's assessment.

Neurotransmitter Signals and You

Neuroscientists can track neurotransmitter signals in the brain. It goes like this: Habitual behavior occurs virtually automatically, without bothering to engage the conscious mind. Neurons fire and travel with inexplicable speed along neurotransmitter pathways formed from repetition.

New behaviors are attempts to revise patterns, so they have no such luxury. Neurons fire without established pathways. It is a much more treacherous journey. Consider walking into your home through your front door. Contrast that with entering through a solid wall on the side of your home, requiring the herculean effort of smashing through to create an alternative workable entryway. This analogy approximates the difference in effort between established habits and revised behavioral patterns.

This may seem a tad demoralizing. Get back here! There is a silver lining.

Taking action close to the point of inspiration greatly increases the probability that a new pattern will in fact be established. Start by noting your intentions. What habit would you like to revise? Confide in a friend or colleague. Writing and verbalizing intentions count as real first steps, instigating the groundbreaking of new pathways.

Once you get a few new neurotransmitter pathways in place, flexing your style while maintaining your comfort becomes easier. The payoff from setting off these miniscule signals can be galactic.

Take Action!
"Arm Fold"

Try this activity to make flexing your style a visceral experience. Stand up without holding anything. (This is the only time I will instruct you to put down this book!) Shake out your arms. Loosen up. Now fold your arms normally, the way you typically fold them. Hold this position for a few moments, noticing how it feels.

Shake out your arms again. Next, fold your arms with the opposite arm on top. Do your best; you may not wholly succeed. Shake out again. For the third round, fold your arms normally again. Last chance to shake out—make the most of it, kick your legs, dance around a bit—no one is looking. Unless you're in the library, in which case you will be encouraging a wait list for this book, which is fine with me.

For the final portion of this experiment, attempt to fold your arms with the opposite arm on top once more.

A. Write three words or phrases to describe what it was like to fold your arms normally, the first time:

1. _____

2. _____

3. _____

B. Now select three words or phrases to describe the experience of folding your opposite arm on top the first time. Write the first three things to come to mind:

1. _____

2. _____

3. _____

C. Was it even slightly easier to fold your opposite arm on top the second time around? Circle one response.

Yes   No   A little bit

D. If folding your opposite arm on top was crucial to your professional success and personal development, could you teach yourself to do it?

Yes   No   A little bit

ANALYSIS

This exercise is a metaphor for flexing your style. When you folded your arms naturally, it was automatic—without conscious intervention. This is the equivalent of behaving within your natural personality style.

When folding your arms with the opposite arm on top, you had to consciously think about how to place your arms and hands. This is the same as practicing new behaviors—testing out alternative responses. When you first practice flexing your style, it feels [insert your responses to B].

Folding your opposite arm on top is easier for some people than for others. An ambidextrous person may have no difficulty at all with this exercise. Similarly, centroverts—those near the border between introvert and extrovert—will find it relatively easy to flex their style. It takes less conscious effort for a centrovert to speak the same language

Notes from the Field
Flex for Success

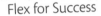

Tanya is a highly regarded senior vice president in a Fortune 100 company. She has remained loyal to her company, steadily and comfortably working her way up the corporate ladder. During an economic downturn, however, her company made it clear that regardless of their role, all executives were expected to bring in business. Tanya had always been uncomfortable soliciting business, so she decided to continue her current practice of high performance in her normal role.

As months passed, she began to recognize the necessity of facing her reluctance to network and sell services. Did she force herself to double her social network, attend every local networking event, schedule daily lunch meetings with vendors, and appear at industry programs weekly? No.

Her carefully executed strategy was a direct departure from traditional networking wisdom. She methodically reviewed her contacts, selecting a single person to approach: a graduate school friend, Mark. She contacted Mark and mentioned that it would mean a lot to arrange a meeting to discuss collaboration between their two businesses. She sincerely believed Mark would also benefit from the alliance, and this conviction came across in their meeting.

Upon reporting her progress to the executive team, she was met with astonishment. It turned out that for years her corporation had wanted to forge a relationship with Mark's company and could never get in the door. A few months later her effort paid off beyond any expectations. Multimillion-dollar contracts were in place, and she is certain this has been her biggest contribution to the company in her twenty-three years there.

as an extrovert or introvert. A person near the far end of the spectrum needs to put more effort into flexing her style. Success is still entirely within reach; temperament indicates preference, not ability.

Another correlation between this experiment and flexing your communication style in general is that it gets easier. If flexing your style matters enough to you, you can learn to fold your opposite arm on top, literally and figuratively.

Talkin' about My Generation

Don't let the song lyrics fool you; I won't talk only about my own generation. I prefer to keep such information hazy, anyway.

Implementation of the Platinum Rule necessitates a sensitivity to those on opposite ends of the I/E continuum, yet plenty of other factors trigger misunderstandings. Generation gaps can cloud our perceptions and trigger misunderstandings. Awareness begets sensitivity, infusing our reactions with a dose of kindness.

GENERATIONAL VARIANCES

Folks get wound up over generational differences. The first step is to *expect* differing preferences rather than being continually confounded by them. Yes, as you suspected, life experiences influence habits. Second, forgive those with styles out of sync with your own. It is neither a deficit nor a personal affront. It is human nature.

For every rule there are exceptions. Yet we will concentrate on widely held behavior to understand tendencies. I agree, all the members of a particular age group are not identical. (But thanks for the reminder.) Early adopters circumvent generational proclivities, enthusiastically embracing emerging technologies. Nevertheless, trends emerge, and recognizing the influence of age groups makes us more tolerant of those from other eras. While year ranges are not universally agreed upon, these are the approximate demographics:

Baby boomer: born 1946–1965

Generation X: born 1966–1980

Millennial: born 1981–1995

iGens—alternatively dubbed Gen Zs—born between 1996 and 2012, are also making their stamp, though the penchants of this cohort are still being defined.

Meeting Attire. Whether heading out to mingle or attending an interview, sensibilities collide. Millennials skew informal, with a sprinkling of fashion trends. Their independent spirits decry societal dress codes. Boomers are the most formally dressed at work, showing up in ties or suits even on "casual Friday." Gen Xers split the difference, prone to donning a jacket over an unbuttoned shirt or comfortable dress. They value ease and practicality.

Business Cards. While "Here's my card" is a networking anchor for baby boomers and many Gen Xers, millennials are more likely to eschew these in favor of electronic alternatives. The savvy millennial will keep snappy cards handy regardless, recognizing that networking takes place intergenerationally.

Follow-up Communication. When reaching out to a new contact, demographics play a part in follow-up behavior. Patterns become ingrained, nearly instinctual. Millennials shoot off a text. Gen Xers are most likely to email. Younger boomers also rely on email, but the oldest may prefer to pick up the phone.

Message Styles. Millennials may not think twice about a smattering of emojis and abbreviations such as TTYL and LMK. Gen Xers integrate them selectively, with closer colleagues. Many boomers are satisfied with :^).

In the Office. Whether in an open-space format or traditional office, millennials are all about screens. It is not unusual to see at least three screens continually on. Gen Xers typically stick to one or two at a time—a phone, tablet, or desktop. The occasional boomer will have a desk devoid of screens while maintaining close ties with a mobile device of choice.

Taking the "Phone" Out of Cell Phone. To millennials, the phone is little more than a rarely utilized app on their smartphone. Many don't bother to set up voicemail or record voice messages. Gen Xers favor written follow-up after networking encounters. Remote conversations are increasingly scheduled and conducted via apps such as Skype, Google Hangouts, and Zoom. Boomers are most likely to use a cell phone as, well, a phone.

Weekends and Holidays. Millennials rarely unplug. Gen Xers work on creating systems to separate work and downtime. Boomers are most apt to be offline on weekends and at ease being off the grid on vacations.

Each of these styles reflects generationally influenced values and habits. Differences can fuel misunderstandings and postulation of subversive motives. No need to get persnickety. The Platinum Rule can counter these tendencies. Understanding the reasons behind behaviors allows you to replace annoyance with appreciation. What works for you doesn't work for everyone.

Preferences are not linked to ability. I beseech you to refrain from inferring capabilities based on age. Younger doesn't mean naïve; older doesn't mean out of touch. Aspire to being age-blind as you network.

BE CAREFUL WHAT YOU WISH FOR

As you tap into your inner networker, others may start gravitating toward you in droves. What once felt impossible, daunting, and dreadful begins to happen effortlessly. Still, be sure to schedule downtime.

> Inner preferences remain largely intact even as outer
> behaviors develop, grow, and adapt.

A plethora of continual interactions, if not carefully managed, will drain introverts. I apparently come across as quite accessible. People I don't know regularly engage me in conversation. It is a bit like being on my own little reality show. Drop an introvert into the world with a giant "Talk to me!" sign over her head and watch what happens.

How do you advise me to handle this? Write your best advice here.

_____

_____

_____

_____

_____

Good. Keep this advice in mind. As you get better at this stuff, you may need to implement this counsel yourself.

WHAT YOU SEE AND WHAT YOU GET

Personality preferences are internal, not easily discernible to an external viewer. An average observer could notice an extrovert and introvert engaged in conversation at an event without picking up on fundamental differences, such as what propelled each to attend. One came to tackle the challenge; the other, because it sounded fun. Guess which?

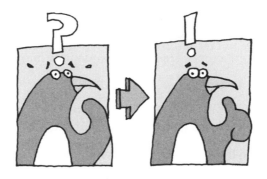

CHAPTER 6

sparkling new strategies

The summit of happiness is reached when a person is ready to be what he is.

—Desiderius Erasmus

It Happens to the Best of Us Quiz

True or False

Drained introverts can be a tad touchy.

Answer:

True. There is no point sugarcoating the reality of the matter. Learn how to network without becoming overwhelmed and exhausted. You will *feel* better and *do* better.

Why does the same advice that makes an extrovert giddy sink like a rock in the stomach of an introvert? Experiences that fill an extrovert with glee make an introvert feel inauthentic and exhausted.

Go ask an extrovert for networking tips. You'll find one nearby, chatting with the others. Her recommendations may include acquiring lots of contacts, meeting as many people as possible, and filling your calendar with events.

An introvert, who foolishly attempts to follow the string of advice blithely offered by an extroverted networking advocate, will collapse faster than a soufflé at a fireworks display. The same traditional rules light up an extrovert like the sky.

Follow your energy. If you turn every meal into a networking opportunity, you will collapse from exhaustion within two weeks.

A drained introvert is an ineffective introvert.

I love to eat alone. In fact, throughout my freshman year in college, my mother would phone to ask if I had eaten lunch with anyone. And because the answer was generally no, for a year she fretted that I had no friends. Upon reading this book she can finally breathe a sigh of relief.

Some things don't change. To this day a solo meal perusing a newsfeed or magazine is an oasis of calm that reenergizes me. On hectic days, even a few restorative minutes help me stay centered. What happens when I schedule zero recharge time? Production goes down, I am wiped out, and the meetings are ineffective.

Be True to You

The nonnegotiable premise of quality networking is to be yourself. Your personality is the foundation on which to build. Attempting to transform yourself into another type of person is a dangerous business that will leave you dazed, confused, and wiped out. I cannot condone such reckless behavior.

We succeed by honoring our strengths, not by denying our temperaments.

Why not revel in who you are? Doesn't that sound a lot more fun, relaxing, and validating? Success starts with being real.

At the start of my career, I attempted to emulate other successful presenters. Rookie mistake. Soon I dropped this approach, broke a lot of rules, and became myself at home *and* at work. I crack jokes, keep it lively, and merge spontaneity with structure. You are how you are for a reason. Being authentic is best thing that can ever happen to you. It also guarantees you'll make the maximum positive impact in the world.

If you are overwhelmed, try to start enjoying the ride instead of dwelling on what you *should* do. *Should* is not very inspiring. In fact, notice when you tell yourself you should engage in some kind of networking behavior. *I should interject myself into that group of people already in conversation. I should stay out late with the others. I should make more small talk at every opportunity.* Perhaps you'll notice that *should* nearly always means you *should not.* You should never say should.

Notes from the Field

Namaste

I take yoga classes populated by introverts and extroverts. Classes end with a relaxing closer, designed to leave participants centered and balanced—reenergized. Upon conclusion, the introverts tiptoe around, not wanting to break the glorious silence. The extroverts? The moment the lights ease on, they burst into lively conversation: "Wasn't that wonderful? I feel so rejuvenated!" Each time, I am reminded of how extroverts express a surge of energy. Words bubble forth.

The old rules are limited. They work for the 15 percent of the population who identify strongly as extroverts. Centroverts and introverts do not benefit from the old rules. Let's take hold of the reins.

Our sparkly new *3-P Strategies* are user-friendly for introverts, centroverts, and even plenty of card-carrying extroverts. The 3-Ps serve those who hate networking, while teaching everyone how to better relate to those with different styles. Moving forward, we'll elaborate and apply to an array of scenarios. Unlike 3-D, no special glasses are required.

Join me in turning three old-school networking premises on their heads. Drum roll, please.

Dusty Old Rule #1: Jump On In (Patter)

Let's face facts: extroverts can talk. Because they verbalize naturally, chatting comes easily. Yo, introverts, stop rolling your eyes! Graciously cede the point. Extroverts talk to think. At times, this defining trait causes boundless aggravation for introverts; other times it spurs envy. They slide into networking mode with ease.

Notes from the Field
Welcome. Now Leave Me Alone!

Among facilitators, it is standard practice to greet participants as they first enter the classroom. Everyone knows the right things to do: introduce yourself, build rapport, and start learning names. We are talking *introductory facilitation procedures* here.

I do the opposite, hiding at the front of the room, face down in my papers. Completely unacceptable behavior for a presenter! At the very least, it is rude. Right?

Not so fast. I need to conserve my energy leading up to the starting gate. I ignore the basic procedure until introduced. Then I flip on my sparkle switch, beam at the audience, and sprint out the gate. Toss the rules. Being true to yourself means everyone benefits.

The ability to maintain a friendly stream of patter enables extroverts to keep a conversation flowing, a discussion lively, and an event afloat. They know it, introverts know it, and we all may as well accept it.

Jumping into conversations is one way to build contacts. Extroverts are quite comfortable talking with virtual strangers—otherwise known as new friends. "A stranger is a friend you haven't met yet" is a purely extrovert credo. Extroverts like spending as much time as possible interacting with others. This is why a socially driven person is well positioned to take the advice of old rule #1 and run with it.

What about everyone else?

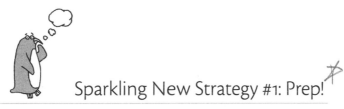

Sparkling New Strategy #1: Prep!

When I ask extroverts to describe introverts' strengths, "good listeners" frequently tops the list. This compliment seems to be an undisputed win for introverts, as extroverts are forthcoming about their own need for development in the same area. Not that it's a competition. As one of my sons likes to say, "It's not a race, but I'm winning."

Introverts are hardwired to think to talk. Owning this truism enables us to turn a potential shortcoming into a skill. Designate planning time to set goals and think through strategies prior to meetings. By implementing our first new networking strategy—*prep*—you can communicate with clarity and precision.

When interacting with others, we learn more from observing than from speaking. If chitchat does not flow forth naturally, focus on what you *do* have—a predisposition for keen observation and thoughtful responses. When networking, introverts flourish by organizing their thoughts, researching options, and formulating plans in advance. We'll explore methods and details in the chapters ahead.

Dusty Old Rule #2: Sell Yourself (Promote)

Self-promotion syncs with the extrovert disposition. Supplementing this aim, networking advice for extroverts promotes a high volume of ongoing interaction. Actual tips I have come across in this arena include:

- Be visible at all times.
- Share accomplishments freely.
- Make every meal a networking opportunity.
- Maintain constant contact.
- Continually update others on your business.

Promotion is a natural extension of an extrovert's disposition. A sincere interest in getting involved provides a diverse platform for selling their services. Quantity and frequency are valued.

A vibrant, extroverted long-time client of mine is a nonprofit executive director. When I told her the name of this book, she laughed. "How could anyone hate networking? It is my favorite part of the job!" She did note, however, that the book would help her better understand the introvert and centrovert team with which she had surrounded herself!

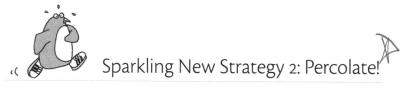 ## Sparkling New Strategy 2: Percolate!

Introverts are unlikely to kick off a relationship by talking about their innumerable fine attributes. However, peak-functioning introverts percolate. They permeate beyond the surface, infuse conversations with depth, display interest in others, and tap into a lively exchange. An introvert can filter through the superficial to learn a tremendous amount about and from others.

Introverts strive for profundity in relationships and experiences. Allow yourself to ease into building connections, using introvert-friendly tactics. Percolating enables introverts to create deeper contacts with remarkably little time spent on self-promotion.

I overheard the following description of a colleague: "She is reserved but has a great deal of depth within her." I noticed the *but*. As if it is contradictory for a reserved person to have depth. I have noticed that people who initially seem taciturn eventually— and often quite suddenly—reveal intriguing backgrounds, talents, and personalities.

Notes from the Field
Still Waters Run Deep

I met Luca while facilitating a leadership retreat for seventy senior attorneys at a luxurious lakeside resort. At dinner, served at large banquet tables, Luca was reserved and quiet.

The second morning took place outdoors and required a good deal of prep work, so I arrived early to get going. Luca was the first participant to arrive, half an hour before the program was scheduled to start. He offered to help and took on his tasks with enthusiasm.

I asked what he had done the previous evening, after dinner, and he self-consciously said he'd sat by the lake, watching the water. Luca confided in an apologetic tone, "I like to sit sometimes and just look at the scenery."

He said small talk exhausts him, that he prefers spending time alone during session breaks. Luca explained his early appearance that morning: he intentionally ate breakfast early, unhindered by well-meaning colleagues joining him.

Luca, now quite chatty, went on to extrapolate his belief that he appears uninteresting to people when they first meet him. In *this* conversation, his depth, humor, and thoughtfulness were evident. I later learned that these very qualities directly contribute to his professional success. Luca held a coveted leadership position, overseeing five other attorneys. He thinks to talk and writes with unusual clarity. Following the program, Luca supplied detailed feedback, complete with reflections and recommendations.

Luca exemplifies classic introvert characteristics. He excels one-on-one. He readily opens up when perceiving a safe situation. His richness is hidden from plain view, making its discovery that much more satisfying. Like many introverts, he has hidden layers. We are richly rewarded when we allow introverts to unfold on their own terms.

If you are an introvert, make the most of your fabulous talents. Introverts are more comfortable asking questions than revealing personal information. Tap into your ability to ask well-formed questions, and you'll never again lose sleep over being at a loss for conversation. Furthermore, your astute attention to subtle nonverbal cues allows you to absorb a tremendous amount about others.

Closed-ended questions generate only a yes or no response. Open-ended questions maximize information. Reword "Do you like your job?" to "What is your favorite part of your job?" Also, *why* tends to put the responder on the defensive. Whenever possible, replace *why* with *how* or *what*. Replace "Why did you leave your job?" with "What led you to make a career change?"

Recall a time you met someone and walked away with a positive impression. Most likely, she demonstrated an interest in *you*. Quality questions build rapport—a slam-dunk for making a strong first impression.

Dusty Old Rule #3: Maximize Time with Others (Party)

This advice plays directly into the first precondition for a visa to Extroland: be social! Extroverts revive their energy by regularly spending lots of time with lots of people.

In conversation with an extrovert, I was surprised to hear her say she enjoyed taking day trips alone. I pressed for details. She clarified, "I hop on a tour bus and spend the rest of the day chatting with whomever happens to be seated next to me. It's great!"

Joining groups and attending gatherings enables extroverts to revitalize their spirits. Holing oneself up in a hotel room on a business trip is counterintuitive and counterproductive for someone who gets an energy infusion from being with others.

Extroverts thrive in environments with abundant activities. If this is you, fill your day, your life, your time with social events galore. There are many variations on this beloved Extroland treatise. Even when relaxing at home, extroverts will have several devices and screens going at once, preferring activity to silence. The more the merrier.

Sparkling New Strategy #3: Pace!

Pace is shorthand for "pace yourself." Why is this important? Introverts and centroverts do best when deeply engaged, whether in conversation, thought, or purposeful action. Enter our third glittering strategy. Pacing yourself means creating a networking schedule that suits your temperament. Honor the amount of networking you can comfortably manage over a period of time while also taking breaks during an event. Build a connection. Retreat to refresh. Repeat.

Wham! Emerge a networking dynamo.

Give Yourself a Time-Out!

The penalty that an unruly three-year-old dreads is a sweet, soothing melody to the overwhelmed, exhausted networker. You are in a time-out!

Because . . . Introverts. Energize. Alone.

We crave being alone. We require I-time to function. It is as basic as that. Introverts revel in this assertion from philosopher Martin Buber:

Solitude is the place of purification.

Successful networking requires acknowledging your strengths and honoring your needs. To maintain your enviable self-reliance, create regular escapes to refuel. A brief stroll, soak in the tub, or ten minutes with a junky novel? They all count.

What a relief. Advice that doesn't make you want to turn on your heel and head for the hills. Plus, it works wayyyy better for introverts than the standard, sundry extro-centric advice.

LESS IS MORE

High-functioning introverts replace quantity with quality. Sure, an introvert could put the pedal to the metal and tough it out. She could dutifully follow advice that endorses devoting all spare moments to networking. The results? Unsatisfying. The introvert? Panting for air.

> **Quantity is an exhausting and inauthentic measurement of success for introverts.**

A solid, compact network of reliable contacts is the best-case scenario for the introvert. When actively networking in this realm, less is more.

> **Less time + Fewer people = Better outcomes**

This equation tasks introverts with meeting, say, one person per event, not ten. Because introverts go deep, numerous simultaneous pursuits overwhelm them. Extroverts can comfortably acquire a wide range of associates, and they are equally fine keeping superficial ties with most. This is unacceptable to introverts, who prefer fewer, more substantive connections. Filling life with a plethora of activities and people snuffs an introvert's flame right out.

I know firsthand how well this strategy works. You truly can achieve top-notch results with less energy. While seeking out a prospective publisher, I did advance research, narrowing my target down to one (one!) ideal option. Rather than wiping myself out pounding the pavement, I had a single meeting at an industry conference. I had done extensive research, and Berrett-Koehler (BK), my publisher of choice, picked up on my authentic enthusiasm. Here we are ten years later: I'm still writing books. And BK has published them all.

Introverts and extroverts have different networking propensities:

> **Extroverts collect. Introverts connect.**

Extroverts flow through the room, casually bantering with whomever they meet. Introverts seek targeted interactions. The upshot? Extroverts collect a bigger stack of cards; introverts connect through deeper conversations. An increased understanding leads to a new appreciation of our opposites and a platform to build rapport across temperaments.

In the chapters ahead, we will apply the concepts of *prep*, *percolate*, and *pace* to all kinds of scenarios, including job searches, business trips, follow-up, and more!

Notes from the Field

In the Spotlight, under the Microscope

I was presenting throughout a three-day conference. My interactive programming required enormous energy. The conference was a hit. However, I failed to pace myself between sessions, constantly dashing from event to obligation and back again.

A couple of weeks later, I received a phone call from my client. She said a participant reported that she approached me after a session (an encounter I didn't recall), and I "blew her off." I felt terrible yet appreciated the feedback. The interaction, I was told, had taken place after the concluding program on the final day. On that day, I was wiped out and poised to sprint to the privacy of my suite. I can imagine conveying a nearly complete lack of presence at that point. In my mind I was already out the door. Luckily, my client knew me well enough to interpret the misunderstanding.

What I learned, and now offer as advice to fellow introverts, is that when you're in the limelight, maintain your presence of mind along with your presence. An unintended offense can become impossible to undo later. Pacing is not a luxury—it is a necessary component of a successful overall strategy.

Extrovert's Principles

Guiding Principle	Supporting Technique	Essence
Talk to think	**PATTER**	Verbal
Seek breadth	**PROMOTE**	Expansive
Energize with others	**PARTY**	Social

Introvert's Principles

Guiding Principle	Supporting Technique	Essence
Think to talk	**PREP**	Reflective
Seek depth	**PERCOLATE**	Focused
Energize alone	**PACE**	Self-reliant

Whether an introvert or extrovert, you're fantastic as is. You are well positioned to win all kinds of networker-of-the-year awards. Start jotting notes for your acceptance speech.

CHAPTER 7

networking event survival kit

Fortune helps those who dare.

—Virgil

Networking Survival Quiz

1. Is *Networking for People Who Hate Networking* an oxymoron?
2. Do extroverts have networking all wrapped up?
3. Can extroverts and introverts peacefully coexist alongside a chocolate fondue fountain?

Answers:

1. No.
2. No.
3. Yes.

Networking events are those special times in life when people gather together, generally in large numbers, to chitchat, exchange contact info, and eat unhealthy, unidentifiable fried food in unnatural quantities.

How is a networking hater to survive, let alone thrive?

When I go to an event, it is either an unavoidable obligation or because I coerced myself. I am frequently pleased with the results, yet I head there under duress.

To me, this is like morning exercise. I've been an early bird at the gym for years. I trick myself—a clue that I'm not so bright. I tell myself things like, *I'll just drive slowly past it today*. Once in the vicinity, I rally. The cycle starts all over again the next day. As I resentfully bash the snooze button, I curse myself. I vow I'll never work out again. Afterward? I feel like a million bucks. Repeat.

Don't wait until you are all psyched to go networking.

Dillydallying until the mood strikes means waiting forever.

You've got to kick yourself out that door. Once there, armed with your secret prep, percolate, and pace (yourself) strategy, you'll do fine. No wimps.

Dragging Yourself There

There's a big corporate event tonight. Attendance is not technically required, although you are expected to go. The change of clothes you brought from home hangs from a hook on your office door. Every time someone comes in or goes out, the garment bag swings, drawing your attention back to the event looming near the end of an exhausting week.

By six o'clock your mind is buzzing from the day's collective sensory bombardment. Miscellaneous meetings, a presentation, the noisy lunchroom, spontaneous hallway exchanges, and a conference call have left you wiped out. You want to decompress. Your mind scans a gamut of excuses, hoping to discover a legitimate reason to bail. You idly begin organizing your files, a task you normally avoid. Now you're going to be late. Realizing it is hopeless, you put on your evening outfit and trudge to the event.

Entering the networking venue, you see unknown people milling around with nametags already peeling off their business suit lapels. The volume is high, and the mood seems cheerful—in direct contrast to your own state. People are upbeat and laughing, perusing picked-over tapas platters. You wonder how much more time is required to fulfill your obligation to attend.

An initial search for officemates proves futile. After being in attendance for three minutes, you hide in a corner to check messages. Another tedious night of networking—or the failure thereof—begins. How about a do-over? Networking, take two.

Prep

Preregister. Commit in advance. You'll be less likely to back down, particularly if you paid to attend. Plus, registration fees often increase at the door. Signing up early also ensures entry to popular events. Not to mention you'll score a professionally rendered preprinted nametag.

Volunteer. Inquire in advance whether you can help in some capacity. Many networking-haters are most comfortable when in a designated, structured role. Volunteering provides you with a specific reason to engage with others, rather than poking around for small talk. Bonus: you position yourself as helpful.

Attire. Weigh the value of comfort versus fashion. Will that flowy scarf, wafting about, become distracting? Do your feet hurt after fifteen minutes in platform heels? Do your contact lenses dry out, making eyeglasses the wiser choice? Is that snappy jacket a tad snug these days? What image do you want to convey? Millennials in particular are at risk of donning overly casual attire at business events. Consider dressing up a notch.

Go with a pal. An ally can transform the experience. Make plans to attend with a networking-adverse colleague. Take turns venturing out and reporting back while giving each other mini networking "assignments." A shared positive attitude and sense of humor will attract others to you both.

Clarify goals. Why are you attending? Set modest, actionable goals, such as meeting two new people. Be realistic. A detailed goal-setting structure can be found in chapter 8.

Arrive early. If you are hesitant to attend an event, why get there first? Because it is better to show up when there are only a few, scattered people than face a noisy crowd, all packed together. Gatherings are cozier and calmer near the beginning. Arriving early also presents an opportunity to see if you can help out.

Take a moment. Center internally and refresh externally. Look in a mirror—best-case scenario is a well-appointed powder room; backup plan is your phone's camera. Check yourself out. Make sure you are at your best, or at least not entirely disheveled. Pop a breath mint. Take a couple of deep, restorative breaths.

Check out the nametags. Upon arrival, glance over the nametags of attendees, often arranged near the entrance in alphabetical order. An early arrival ensures that most have not yet been picked up, allowing you to anticipate attendance of those you know or want to meet. It also provides I-time before crowds ensue.

Scan the room. Position yourself somewhere between the outskirts and the inner circles to obtain a good view of the maximum number of attendees. No mathematical formulas are necessary. Conduct a slow visual scan of the room. Look for those you know and those who, for whatever reason, seem approachable.

See how you are being gently eased into actual human contact?

 Percolate

Be an open target. Make yourself approachable. Consciously maintain a pleasant expression. Standing-only tables are magnets for solitary folks open to conversation. Find an open table where you can comfortably hang out or join another solo whose nonverbal cues indicate he is open to company.

Visit the information tables. Event organizers often display information about products or services. Perusing pamphlets allows you to learn about your hosts, come up with relevant conversation starters, and interact with those working the tables.

Make eye contact. Eye contact conveys an interest in others, increasing their positive perception of you. It's a nonverbal way to initiate connections, especially when accompanied by a friendly smile. Restrain yourself from glancing around at the crowd while engaged in conversation. Eye contact disciplines you to pay attention, edging out unrelated thoughts and negative self-talk. Just don't overdo it with a scary stare-down.

Acknowledge and thank staff. This extends beyond those running the event to include bartenders, coat room attendees, and anyone else working the venue. It is good form to show appreciation. Be prepared to tip. An open bar does not necessarily cover tips.

Get in line. Lines provide a fine alternative to standing around alone. Conversation openers with fellow line-mates include asking about work, the origin of an interesting name, or what brought them to the event. You even earn a prize: whatever you were standing in line for. Completing your time in the line provides a built-in closer—exchange contact information and be on your way.

Be gracious. Before getting a drink, ask whether anyone nearby would like something too. When standing in line for a buffet, hand a plate to the person behind you and offer to let him go ahead. You get the idea.

Note the unusual. Notable accessories or unique styles invite conversation. People tend to purchase and wear distinct items to make a statement. You can't go wrong complimenting and inquiring about these items, as long as you keep it real.

Linger by the crudités. Food stations are a fine jump start for conversation while also providing a temporary place and purpose. As others arrive, many one-liners are at your disposal, such as:

- Nice selection! (Only if there are more than two food groups)
- Do you know what type of cheese this is? (Best if not pointing to cheddar)
- What do you think of the freshly made pasta?
- Such a creative dessert display—what's your favorite?

Take small enough bites to be able to respond to others without an awkward time lapse for chewing. And choking is a major faux pas.

Notes from the Field
Eat Before, Drink After

If this tip seems stodgy, rest assured I'm not a fan, either. Yet I'm doing you a solid. It is tempting to gleefully go to town at an event. If you paid to attend, you want to get your money's worth, and if you did not, hey, it's a free meal. Nevertheless, arriving ravenous plops you into a high-risk danger zone. To name a few: seeds from artisan flatbread stuck in your teeth; cramming in a mouthful of spinach salad a nanosecond prior to someone's asking your name; taking on the odor of garlic-infused meatballs; and spilling while juggling a plate, glass, and handshake.

I'm not suggesting you eat nothing. Be selective and moderate. This is easiest when you've taken the edge off prior to the event with, say, an energy bar, some fruit, a handful of nuts—ideally a snack featuring protein and energy. At the event, stick to small portions, easy-to-manage bites, and simple options.

On to drinking "adult beverages." I'm frequently informed by earnest sippers, "I network much better after a few drinks." To this I reply, "Says you. Let's poll the others in attendance, shall we?" Errors in judgment, some impossible to undo, rise exponentially with the quantity of drinks consumed. If you relish a cocktail, be moderate: two per event, with a hydrator between. You're not attending your first frat party and dipping into a bottomless vat of mysterious punch.

Be clear on the difference between pals and colleagues. Going out when off the clock doesn't give you free rein to let loose with new acquaintances or long-time colleagues. You don't want to be Monday morning's water cooler story

Focus on others. Chatting with strangers can be challenging. The most common reason being *I have no idea what to talk about!* Get this: you don't have to! Displaying an interest in others makes you more likeable than regaling them with details of your latest exploits. Jackpot! Thoughtful questions are the place to start. Some sample openers:

- What do you like best about your work?
- What interesting projects are you working on?
- What's been the highlight of your year?
- Want to join me in checking out the displays?

Focus on you. Artfully directing all conversation away from your carefully guarded self can go too far. One-way conversations can segue into imbalanced relationships. Be prepared to offer up a few tidbits about yourself. Choose in advance a few topics you are comfortable sharing, enabling others to get to know you, too.

Pace

Regularly recharge. Socializing depletes an introvert's energy reserves. Sensory overload makes energy vanish faster than an open lane on Santa Monica Boulevard. Head out for a breather, step away to decompress, or take a brief walk.

Maintain Perspective. Keep in mind that only you know how long you linger outside taking in the view, how often you visit the powder room, or how many people you meet. No one else is keeping track—unless you do something supremely embarrassing. We won't dwell on this counterproductive thought.

End conversations gracefully. This valuable skill ensures that conversations don't fizzle out past their prime. It is tempting to stick around when enjoying a conversation, but better to wrap it up prior to running out of things to talk about and the onset of awkward pauses.

If you love someone, set them free!

Offer your new compatriot an out. She is here to circulate and may not want to chat too long with one companion, however pleasant the exchange. You need to get back out there too, and now you are buoyed by an early networking victory. Warmth is a component of successful closure. To get started, check out these ideas:

- May I have your card? It was great meeting you.
- I am headed over to get something to eat/drink.
- Have you met [colleague passing by]?
- I'm going to freshen up.
- I need to make a call.
- I've enjoyed our conversation! Thank you.
- I look forward to following up.
- I promised myself I'd circulate. Enjoy the event!
- I'd like to get some fresh air.
- I'm going to sit down for a bit.
- I really have to go. I'd love to stay in touch.
- I'm sure you want to talk with others; I won't hold you up.

It goes without saying you have your cards with you everywhere you go. And if you claim to be headed somewhere, *really go* (nothing like trashing your credibility immediately).

Know when to split. Set a reasonable predetermined sayonara time. Sorry, ten minutes post-arrival doesn't qualify. Muscle through the first half-hour to acclimate; sometimes it takes a little perseverance to get into your groove. Clock out when you have accomplished your goals—and before you feel like you're swirling around a giant drain.

Notes from the Field
Three Cards

Following a networking event, an introverted client excitedly reported back to me that she had collected three cards. To an extrovert, this is a pittance. Yet my client remembered the conversations and sent friendly, specific notes such as "I enjoyed our conversation about your recent, inspiring professional successes . . ." She extended offers to meet for coffee; two accepted. A year later she remained in touch with both and did business with one.

Plan your escape. Have a departure plan. It's best if you're not dependent on someone else's timeframe. If you are tied into others' schedules, find a quiet place to wait as they finish up. Refrain from loitering by the door.

Keep the momentum. Consider that quarterly potluck your team coordinates. The one you are running out of feasible excuses to avoid. Rally and show up. It is remarkable what out-of-office interactions can do for rapport and productivity. Focus on nonwork topics. Otherwise, you might as well be at an ordinary staff meeting.

Nametags 'n You

Turns out I have developed myriad opinions about nametags. Some people occupy their minds with lofty topics such as philosophy, politics, or sports scores. I am lost in the trenches of nametags. The benefit of this preoccupation is to share with you my heavily considered insights.

Prioritize. If your preprinted nametag has inaccurate information, how important is a correction? Fixing the information probably means replacing a prepared nametag with a handwritten version. If it is a misspelling of your name (Michele instead of Michelle or Christy in place of Christi), you might decide to let it slide. If there is an incorrect title, not accurately reflecting a recent promotion, this may be worth fixing.

Print. When situations require writing your own nametag, use the thickest marker available. Print your first name clearly in large capitals with your last name and title smaller beneath. Do not crowd your nametag with extraneous information. If you make a mistake, throw it out and start afresh. A messy nametag is unreadable and unprofessional. Take a moment; it becomes the most important thing you are wearing.

Plastic. A nametag in a plastic sleeve is a great thing. I put a small supply of my business cards behind the name card, inside the plastic sleeve. They are easily accessible, neatly in one place, and carried hands-free. You can also use this spot to stash the cards of others you meet.

Be creative, within your comfort zone.

Conversation Management

There are endless questions that introverts deem private but extroverts think nothing of asking a total stranger. How to respond? Reserve judgment and try to not take offense. After all, you don't want an extroverted coworker taking your own boundless need for privacy personally, do you? Prepare responses to high-frequency questions. Here's a list, followed by adaptable replies.

To be clear, these are questions you might be asked, not ones I recommend initiating.

- How long do you plan on working here?
- How much did that [fill in the blank] cost?
- What is your salary?
- Do you have a family?
- Do you like [that person]?
- How old are you?
- Who did you vote for?
- Are you religious?
- What is your opinion on [divisive current event]?
- Why do you think [that person] really got promoted?
- What do you really think of [this place/your company]?

Potential, mostly interchangeable, replies:

- It is hard to say. And you?
- I don't remember.
- I can't recall the last time I checked.
- I'd rather not get into that.
- It's relative.
- I can't go into all that now.
- I try not to think about it.
- I'd have to think about that.
- I haven't been here long enough.
- What do *you* think?
- Not my favorite topic of conversation.
- [Shrug] Want to grab something from the buffet/bar?
- Oh, that! [Sigh.] Let's talk about something else.

A positive demeanor and lighthearted tone are crucial accompaniments to the above. If you feel uncomfortable, select a closer from the "End conversations gracefully" segment earlier in this chapter. Be cheerful and firm. You're on your way.

Notes from the Field

Clumsy . . . or Clever?

Following the publication of the first edition of *Networking for People Who Hate Networking*, I was invited to tour Australia. While conducting a networking seminar, I shared a variety of tips, then invited attendees to share their own networking tactics.

A spirited woman jumped up and bestowed on us her favorite, and certainly memorable, strategy. "Standing near the middle of the crowd, I dump a bunch of my business cards on the ground around me. I make it look like an accident. As people rush to help me gather the cards, they can't help but look at what's written on them. This prompts reactions such as, "Oh, you're in real estate! How interesting; tell me about your work." While I can't exactly advocate her antics, she's got spunk.

CHAPTER 8

without a net:
beyond networking events

If there is no wind, row.

—Latin proverb

Question: What personality type is most in danger of being dubbed snobbish?

Answer:

A confident introvert who does not join in on conversations.
Others, confused, are prone to label her a rude extrovert.

Structure Success

Brace yourself. I have good news and bad news, and it is the same news:

Life is one giant networking opportunity.

I understand that if you already consider yourself overwhelmed, this proclamation is unlikely to help matters. Breathe into a paper bag to reestablish your equilibrium. Panic will get you nowhere. Luckily, most of life is not a networking *event.*

Networking doesn't take place only at a designated time and place. For better or worse, it is an ongoing state. At first glance, this may seem "for worse" to a network avoider. You do not get to check networking off your list of things to do and crawl back under your cozy rock. Even so, this could be your lucky day. You don't need to rely purely on networking happy hours to forge connections. Every place you go and person you meet has potential.

Each encounter is an opportunity.

 Prep

People who dislike traditional networking functions do well attending programs with a clear format and intrinsic purpose. Good choices? Take a class, attend educational seminars, participate in a forum, sign up for a lecture series, or participate in a community service program. An introverted colleague told me she will attend only structured events, avoiding loosely configured networking gatherings whenever possible.

Take Action!
"Personal Inventory"

Now is a fine time to take inventory of circumstances in which you flourish. If not now, when? Situations that support your strengths position you well.

1. Recall past experiences in which you were at your peak. Examples can be professional or personal; a range is good. Make an unfiltered list—it needn't satisfy your left brain's propensity for logic or even seem relevant. Notate three in the first column.

Previous Successful Situation	What Made It Work	Potential Future Opportunity
1.		
2.		
3.		

2. Review your lists. In the second column, assess what helped you thrive. Examples may include having a specific role, doing an enjoyable activity, being intellectually stimulated, conquering a physical challenge, enjoying a novel experience, or learning something new.

3. In the third column, list one or more potential new situations that meet the criteria identified in column two. Here's an example of a completed row:

I volunteered at an international conference.	I had a designated role in a field I care about. Having a defined status made it easier to talk to others. There were opportunities to both help and learn.	I could investigate joining a local nonprofit board. I will have a purposeful role and make connections while contributing to a valuable cause.

The original and future opportunities are different, yet the second is modeled on what worked in the first. In this case, serving on a local board provides an ongoing networking platform. Being clear on your intended outcome determines the next logical step. If your goal is to find a new job, and you want to work in the arts, you might explore offerings at nearby museums or concert halls. If you are an electrical engineer specializing in high-tech firms and looking for a job, your third column may read, "Locate a local association for electrical engineers. Volunteer at an event, and if it's a good fit, get more involved."

Saying No

Your carefully honed antinetworking predisposition protects you from inadvertently stumbling into networking opportunities. It's time to rethink this strategy.

Introverts are a bit inclined to say no before yes. What is the reason for this phenomenon? Why are introverts likely to reject unexpected requests, prospects, and changes? Don't get all defensive; I notice this inclination in myself, too. I am having a laugh right now, envisioning you stifling the urge to insist "No! That's not true!"

The reason behind this tendency is that introverts need to process. When approached with a new idea without time to think it over, introverts are predisposed to respond with a quick "No." There is a way around this. When presenting a concept to a suspected introvert, don't let her respond immediately. Offer the idea, then fly out the door, saying "Let's discuss it later." You may be surprised at her receptivity when you return in a couple of hours. Welcome to a personality behaviorist's version of a geometrical theorem.

A. Introverts prefer to weigh many angles before committing to a response.
B. If not given time to craft a thoughtful reply, an introvert's kneejerk reaction is to reject unanticipated change.
C. If you spring a new idea on an introvert followed by the prompt "Are you on board?" the initial response is likely to be negative.

If A = B and B = C then A = C.

What to do with this insight? There is no use getting agitated or taking the theorem personally. Accept that introverts may require extra time to process new ideas. And on the receiving end:

1. Anticipate and capture "No" before it escapes your lips. Say instead that you will consider the suggestion and get back to that person.
2. Request, when appropriate, that others submit ideas to you in written form. Time to think allows an introvert to prepare and respond with a thoughtful opinion.
3. When under fire, pause before verbalizing your response. Saying "Let me take a moment" conveys that you're giving it thought, not spacing out.

By managing your proclivity to initially reject unanticipated suggestions—such as invitations to get out there and meet new people—you open the gateway to broader possibilities.

 ## Percolate

As we discovered via the Platinum Rule, calibrating your style puts others at ease. Being tuned in to another's comfort zone also builds rapport. What can increase your likelihood of a positive encounter? You may not bat a thousand, but here are some hints.

Advice for Introverts!	**Advice for Extroverts!**
■ If you want lunch one-on-one with an extrovert, make that clear, so she doesn't spontaneously bring someone else along.	■ Silence from an introvert does not correlate with disdain for an idea. She could be thinking it over.
■ When under time constraints, refrain from asking extroverts extraneous questions. You may be treated to a lengthy and avoidable exposition.	■ When faced with a quiet person, do not wonder *What's his problem?* You may be in the presence of an introvert who is engaged yet processing.
■ You may have a colleague who expresses strong opinions, promptly discounted the next day. Rather than label him unreliable, recognize he is thinking aloud, not committing to a future plan.	■ Does your colleague stubbornly stick to his opinions? As introverts ponder and commit to ideas before speaking, it takes more effort to change their minds. Provide time to recalibrate before requesting a response.

You make about a billion choices each day. That is a ballpark estimate. Try to count your choices—conscious and subconscious—and message me with feedback on my approximating skills. That way we don't have to converse directly.

Reminds me of an email sent after my first edition from an appreciative reader in New York. He'd enjoyed the book, and inquired if we could meet at a café if I was ever passing through. He clarified, "We could each bring magazines, so we wouldn't have to talk to each other." What's not to love?

Practice replacing habitual reactions with revised and improved options. Purchase a brand-new set of choices today with free shipping and handling. Possibilities abound. Consider these options and adapt to suit. Edit, delete, reframe.

Notes from the Field
The Perfect Day

In some programs, I sort participants into temperament teams and instruct them to write down what they would do on an ideal day off. Extroverts immediately shout out queries such as, "Can we make the list all together? Can we go on the day together?" Having met a moment earlier, they're prepared to share an idyllic day. I respond that it is up to them. They breathe a sigh of relief and brainstorm a lengthy list of events, laughing, interrupting, and raising the decibel level of the room.

When I ask this group which activities on their list involve others, they boisterously call out, "All of them!" Their faces show that they think this an absurd question. A day alone isn't fun. On their perfect day they are surrounded by friends, concluding with a party.

The introverts nearly always present a short list of solitary pursuits. When asked what activities listed involve other people, it is their turn to laugh. The typical reply? "None." Similar responses can appear on both lists (say, watching a movie, hiking, a leisurely meal). The difference is whether they prefer to engage in these activities alone or with others.

Centroverts—those in the middle of the I/E continuum—create their own group, and, true to type, their activities are a mix of time alone and with others. A distinction is that centroverts more frequently specify who comes along (such as "my best friend") while extroverts are more general and incorporate more people (such as "a pool party").

Why fight reality? Accept where you are and who you encounter. Who are you with? That's who you are supposed to be with at this precise moment. How do you know? What proof do you have? The fact that this person is in front of you. You can bang your head against the wall—or smile charmingly and make it your business to figure out how this encounter factors into your life, on a minor or major scale.

Show, Don't Tell

Small, kind gestures are an alternative to small talk. Actions speak loud and clear. Let others decide you're a genuinely cool person, saving you the trouble of having to mention it yourself. Being on the lookout for ways to be positive and useful also redirects your attention from yourself to others.

Thoughtfulness sets you apart. The following examples take few words to initiate and easily spark a conversation in a range of situations.

- Inquire about an interesting job.
- Seek details about a recent accomplishment.
- Compliment special qualities (bright smile, warmth, positive energy).
- Introduce people you know to each other.
- Honor others' preferences (standing or sitting, inside or outside).
- Maintain a calm exterior when faced with unexpected change.

Say only what is sincere, and follow through on what you promise.

Music to My Ears

Back in college, the first extracurricular activity I pursued was becoming a disc jockey (DJ) on the campus radio station. I love music and thought being a radio DJ would be a great release from college studies. You may foolishly believe DJ'ing is for extroverts. If so, you've never been inside a college radio station transmission room. You sit alone for two- to four-hour shifts and play music. There is a vague sense of others listening to the music remotely, but you exist in your own little universe: a small booth of music. You have time during the songs to plan on-air patter between sets. For an introvert who derives energy from music, this was a haven. Even when I carried the weight of the world in with me—or at least the weight of the campus library—I invariably left revitalized.

A natural progression from the station booth for college DJs is the frat party. Isn't that taking the well-adjusted introvert thing a bit far? Isn't a frat party the ultimate extrovert mosh pit? Well, yes. That's why I rarely attended frat parties. Except as the DJ. While DJs are central to a party, let's take a closer look. The DJ has a clear place and a specific role. DJs need not make small talk or even talk at all, wearing headphones most of the time. As the DJ, you are comfortably alone at a party. In charge of the music, you get to people watch and—amazing for a college student—you are paid to be there! Pretty swank college job. Plus, a surefire conversation starter for years to come.

Compare being a DJ with other roles at a party—like bartending. This person is expected to make continuous small talk with no time alone. See the difference? DJ'ing a party may not top the standard list of introvert-friendly backdrops, yet it includes a clear responsibility: making people happy with fantastic music. Think outside the box for introvert-friendly opportunities.

Pace

Contrary to urban legend, introverts are as likely as extroverts to be effervescent, exuberant, and quick-witted. These traits are often hidden beneath a smooth exterior, exposed when the introvert is at ease and comfortable. You gotta peel away a lot of leaves to get to the heart of an artichoke. (I figure this is a better analogy than an onion, which smells and has nothing special in the middle. Work with me here.)

Extroverts often express pleasant surprise at the person eventually revealed beneath an introverted colleague's protective layers. *Wow! He is really interesting,* they note, once they learn how patience can coax forth an introvert's bloom.

The key to letting the inner you shine forth? Spending time behind the scenes recuperating from being "on."

Speaking of *on* . . .

Online Networking

Does online networking count? To an extent. Does it fulfill your monthly networking quota? No. Hunkering down alone while sending out connection requests doesn't count as all done. Recall our original definition of networking:

Real networking is connecting.

An online presence can contribute to the goal of creating meaningful, lasting connections, serving as a platform or conduit to connect. Applying for jobs in early phases is often virtual and certainly efficient. It is soooo easy with the tap of a key to send your resume to hundreds of potential employers. There is, of course, a hitch. It is equally simple for everyone else; your resume arrives in a sea of thousands. It is supremely difficult to stand out or make a lasting connection.

There is no substitute for real-life encounters. With messaging we get only the words. It's like reading a script in place of attending a play or film. The phone permits cadence and tone to mosey along for the ride. Face-to-face, we are privy to the scope of another's presence. In person we benefit from body language, eye contact, facial expressions, and spontaneous connection.

A decidedly practical client scored a new job in a competitive industry. She quickly developed a strategy to build coalitions with execs in her subsidiary's parent company: "I make friends with them."

I pressed for details.

"I meet them in person. We talk, have a meal together, and afterward we understand each other much better."

Her efforts paid off: She immediately began closing more deals than anyone else on her team.

MESSAGE ME

Voicemail started off as a big deal. Faxes were like magic. Now we risk whiplash from all the new ways to communicate without sitting in the same room. New methods pop up with the verve of pop-ups on our many screens.

I approach the listing of contemporary trends with judicious apprehension that they will have become hopelessly outdated by the time we go to press. Cutting-edge iconoclast today, retro flashback tomorrow. To prove or disprove my point, here are currently popular (some edgy, some waning) platforms for instant messaging: Facebook Messenger, Slack, Google Chat, and Snapchat. In the future you can time travel back to me, technology permitting, and let me know WhatsApp!

At the time of publication, LinkedIn is the go-to forum for professional networking, with up-and-coming subcategories such as ReferHire nipping at its heels. If you're in a relatively conventional line of work, it's a good idea to be at least moderately active and current on LinkedIn or an emerging alternate of your choosing. Remember to:

- Accompany your profile with a photo. A blank space or random logo is suspect.
- Invest in a professional, high-res headshot. Nothing says amateur like a fuzzy selfie.

- Seek and post recommendations from diverse, trusted sources.
- Endorse others' talents and offer to be a referral for your top contacts.
- Send well wishes for connections' milestones.
- Infuse your updates with postings that laud others' accomplishments.

These are great activities on days you take a break from actively networking.

Exploring beyond traditional networking programs is a viable strategy. Amid all these options, stepping away and creating time to *not* network can boost your success even further. Particularly if you devote as little as a half-hour to goal setting.

Outcome Goals

Why is achieving a big-ticket goal often an elusive endeavor? Earnest intentions get us to the starting gate. The crux of the matter is that most goals are poorly formed. You don't have a character flaw; you need a system. Much easier to remedy. Outcome goals* to the rescue!

This system is the finest version of goal setting out there, consistently yielding lasting, positive results. Crave a case study? I was coaching Carlos, a senior executive in a large corporation. He was respected and successful. Still, he felt on the outskirts and wanted to improve his networking aptitude.

In place of a proclamation to try harder, we produced a plan. Carlos worked in a different city from the one where he lived and was committed to his job. Each weekday he arrived early, worked diligently, left to exercise, and returned to his rented apartment. An introvert

---

*Outcome goals are rooted in neuro-linguistic programming (NLP), a cognitive science focusing on enhancing effectiveness through an increased conscious use of our verbal and kinesthetic communication.

with a solid family life on the weekends, he was mostly satisfied with this arrangement.

He believed his career would benefit from expanding his professional network. As an introvert, Carlos felt drained by lengthy group interactions. However, with proper I-time, conversing one-on-one was an ideal platform for his lively warmth.

Challenges are subjective. We decided an achievable stretch goal for Carlos would be to initiate a lunch or coffee break with business associates he didn't know well, twice a month for three months. We even created a chart for him to check off. I am a big believer in adapting sticker charts for grown-up use. They've been around this long for a reason. There's something satisfying about notating accomplishments in little boxes.

What if his goal had been a broad "to get out more"? Such a goal would be sure to fail. Why? It is not measurable. We blame ourselves, citing lack of willpower or conviction. The real culprit is an imprecise goal, unattainable from the start. How do you know if you were successful? You don't. No wonder we get demoralized when aspiring to establish new patterns. Yet thanks to this system, Carlos accomplished his goal while instilling new habits of reaching out to others.

Outcome goals encompass five elements, setting the stage for lasting behavioral change.

POSITIVE

State goals in the positive. As noted on page 44, the brain can never *not* do something; it can only *do* something. Every goal can be rewritten from the negative to the positive. "I am going to stop avoiding networking functions" does not work. "I will attend two networking events in the next four months" does.

CONTROL

While humans are interconnected and rely on others for various resources, a well-formed goal is reasonably within your realm of control. A poorly formed goal requires changes in others' personalities, acts of nature, skill sets fundamentally beyond your realm, or more effort from others than from yourself.

CONTEXT

A well-constructed goal strikes a balance between challenging and achievable. If I believe a goal is impossible, I will not try. If I think a goal is a piece of cake, I'm equally uninspired. "Stretch goals" maximize motivation by eliciting the greatest effort.

ECOLOGICAL

Your life is its own ecosystem. An aspiration can throw everything out of sync if it causes an imbalance. Harmonious goals complement other key aspects of your life, such as sleep, health, or personal relationships. An admirable ambition, not currently sustainable, may be well-suited to an alternative time and place.

MEASURABLE

Think of yourself as a detective. Seek out clues to measure goal accomplishment. Think, *What evidence will let me know I succeeded?* Specificity is the hallmark of attainable goals. *I will expand my network* becomes *I will sign up today for the annual industry conference in May and make travel arrangements immediately.* Either you do or you don't. It's hard to fake it.

Take Action!
"Outcome Goals"

A template for your exclusive use.

Answering these questions lays the groundwork:

What do I want? How can setting an outcome goal contribute to my success? _____

_____

_____

OUTCOME GOAL COMPONENTS

A. **State the outcome positively.** You can more successfully move toward something you want than away from something you do not want.

My goal is: _____

_____

B. **Ensure that the outcome is within your control.** Outcomes that rely excessively on external resources are not well formed.

Do I have the necessary resources to initiate and maintain the outcome? If not, what support, skills, or materials do I need to obtain?

_____

_____

C. **Put your outcome in context.** The outcome ought to be of appropriate size and scope. We are most committed to aspirations that take grit.

Where, when, and with whom will I achieve my outcome?

_____

_____

D. **Choose an outcome that is ecological.** Synchronize goals with your other commitments. Consider the consequences of perusing a goal in the context of what else matters to you.

What will I need to give up or take on to achieve my outcome?

_____

_____

E. **What is a sensory-based, measurable description of your outcome?** Know the "proof" of an achieved goal. Describe the outcome as specifically as possible.

What evidence will I have that my goal has been obtained? How will a successful outcome look, sound, and feel?

_____

_____

Once you've established your goal, commit to an immediate initial action.

My first step, within one week, is . . .

_____

_____

Taking an action right away jump-starts the transformation of intention into change. Our world is filled with many more great beginners than great completers. I have a hunch you're one of the elites.

This awesome framework can be applied to virtually any type of goal setting.

And remember, sharing goals increases their effectiveness. Telling others about your plan solidifies your commitment, builds support, and increases accountability. Introverts, I understand that this is a challenge, yet consider opening up to one or two confidants. Most likely, you'll be glad you did.

CHAPTER 9

the job search

It is so simple to be wise. Think of something stupid to say, and don't say it.

—Sam Levenson

Role Reversal Quiz

When do introverts and centroverts talk a blue streak in job interviews?

Answer:

When they are underprepared.

Seeking employment makes some people self-conscious, causing them to conceal their situation. Regardless of temperament, this will not do. Place shame and blame on the back burner and treat job hunting as a job itself.

I had an influential boss early in my career who said, "When looking for a job, I'll climb the highest hill in town and call out as loud as I can, 'Theo needs a job!!'" Rather than hide unemployment, he taught us to spread the word near and far. Voilà! Everyone you meet becomes your personal job agency, potential fast-tracks to your Next Big Thing. Introverts, I know what you're thinking. But it's worth it.

Years ago, it wasn't uncommon to work for the same company for thirty-plus years. Today that's a rarity. Translation? Virtually everyone you run into has been between jobs at least once, including being downsized, laid off, let go, fired, or RIF'ed.*

There are shifts in marketplace demands and career changers. You are absolutely not alone.

Furthermore, many highly successful, independent professionals—freelancers, salespeople, artists, contractors, consultants—are in perpetual job search mode.

Snap Judgments

Recall a time when you extrapolated a complete set of values based on a momentary exchange. Perhaps you were in an airport, elevator, waiting room, or traffic jam. You saw a person in action. Your inner monologue kicked into high gear, and you brilliantly summed up a stranger's entire persona in less time than it takes to miss a subway stop.

---

*RIF: Reduction in workforce.

Our brains are hardwired to categorize. We observe, collect data, and form conclusions. *His briefcase is spilling out everywhere: he is a mess. She is talking loudly on her phone: she is disrespectful. He is checking out his reflection in the window: must be vain.*

I've got news for you, sugarplum. You aren't the only one jumping to conclusions as if attending the bungee-cord world championships. You too, are on the receiving end of snap judgments. What's a job seeker to do?

Be aware of what you can—and can't—control. You can't control others' perceptions. You *can* bring along the best version of yourself wherever you go. Outer-directed folks are more naturally attuned to external appearances, so ask a pal whose style you admire for friendly tips. He can provide ideas to enhance how you present. Be equally scrupulous about your online presence. Don't be fooled by the presumed distinction between professional and social sites. It is common practice for potential employers or other professional contacts to research postings on primarily social platforms. Use discretion.

Coming up: subterfuge stereotypes and focus on first impressions.

Prep

The best, most versatile networking technique is—a smile. You look skeptical. Hear me out. Smiling . . .

1. . . . is nonverbal. Translation: requires *no talking*! Woo-hoo!
2. . . . sidesteps the sand trap of seeming standoffish.
3. . . . conveys confidence. People who smile are perceived as secure.
4. . . . puts others at ease. Smiles are welcoming.
5. . . . makes you happy. Scientific experiments have shown this is true—emotions follow actions.

Malcolm Gladwell's A+ book *Blink: The Power of Thinking Without Thinking* presents scientific studies that demonstrate "Emotion can . . . start on the face." Gladwell explains that the act of smiling can trigger a positive mood, not just the other way around.

Perhaps you are thinking:

- I am not the smiley type.
- I can't smile if it's not real.

Thanks for leveling with me. However, no free passes today. Consciously summoning a smile before entering a room has a higher payback and lower cost than any other accessory under the sun. Low risk, high return. Think of something happy and make it real. Snap to it.

Complainers never prosper.

Notes from the Field

Just Desserts

In some keynotes, I start by asking participants to identify someone in the room they do not know. Ideally someone they've never even seen before. With writing utensils and paper in hand they partner off, avoiding conversation prior to instructions.

I tell the newly formed pairs they have a total of sixty seconds to talk to each other about their favorite desserts. Halfway through I signal to switch who is talking. At sixty seconds I halt the dialogues and instruct them to write three words or phrases that describe their partner, based solely upon these brief interactions. Whatever comes to mind first. I offer sample ideas (*curious, decisive, spunky, concise* . . .) to help out. Then partners share their descriptors and give reality checks by letting each other know how they did.

At this point, I ask for a show of hands for how many people think their partners did a good job identifying three words to describe them. Consistently, virtually every hand in the room is raised. And while the descriptors are generally positive, they are not generic or interchangeable. One person elicits the term upbeat, another is laid-back.

Among thousands of participants in my programs, from far-reaching industries, nationalities, and walks of life, no one has ever refused to select three words to describe a complete stranger after listening to this person describe a favorite dessert for thirty seconds! So readily do people form first impressions that everybody picks three words, even based on that very limited data. This activity demonstrates:

- People form first impressions lightning fast.
- People's initial perceptions can be remarkably accurate.
- Making a positive impression on others has more value than sizing them up.
- Words and actions help us categorize behaviors and generalize patterns.

When the partner says, "There are so many delicious desserts I could never pick a favorite," we recognize that the person may not be terribly decisive. When another describes the way the frosting looks, we realize he attends to details. When a third gets teary reminiscing about a favorite aunt's apple pie, we understand she is sentimental—or a really big fan of pie.

At times first impressions are nearly instantaneous, even superseding the first utterance. Conversations are . . . icing on the cake.

First impressions are made lickety-split. How difficult is it to prove them wrong? A flurry of research on how long it takes to undo first impressions resulted in a range from "eight more meetings" to "nearly impossible" to "you can't." Therefore, the definitive answer is between eight and infinity meetings.

The number I was taught in business school is two hundred—it takes about two hundred times the amount of information to undo a first impression as it takes to make one. That is a pretty big number, in case you didn't notice. You assess the type of person I am in a flash. Yet if you rapidly determine I'm rude, dull, or generally a mess, I have to put in two hundred times more effort to disprove your belief. We well know I may not merit all those extra opportunities. *Especially* if you are lazy, be certain to make a good first impression! A shortcut toward this modest goal? Display an interest in others.

The bonus is the *halo effect*. If I like one thing about you—say, your friendly smile—my subconscious transfers and expands this information. You develop a lovely invisible halo over your head as I determine that I like most everything about you! I conclude that you are bright, a good team player, kind, thoughtful, funny, and dedicated. There is a big payoff for a positive first impression.

And Now a Bit about You

Self-promotion while job hunting may seem daunting or unsavory. No worries. Plan before you talk (prep), write and practice a very short "advertisement" about yourself (percolate), and have this micro-speech ready to go when needed (pace). Like the best TV ads or movie trailers, don't attempt to tell all. Entice; make people want to learn more.

Have you attended hard-core networking events with an open microphone? Attendees each get thirty seconds to tell everyone else about themselves. Although the opportunity makes some people blanch just thinking about it, the concept is solid. The question is— what would you say? What about situations when people inquire about you? Are you prepared? If not, this next exercise is essential. Thank me later, no rush.

Meet the *thirty-second elevator pitch* (yes, you may have heard about this). Perhaps you prefer the five-minute-ramble-about-myself speech. That will not do. Brevity is more effective and appealing. You know this from being on the receiving end.

Many people do not bother to take the time to create a pitch, figuring they'll wing it. This is downright irresponsible, foolish, and shortsighted. You do not belong in that group. The term *elevator pitch* has its origins in a hypothetical scenario: You find yourself on an elevator with a person of influence. To your surprise, she turns to you and asks, "What do you do here?" This ride is your first and possibly singular opportunity to have her full attention. What happens?

I've been privy to awe-inspiring stories about the impact of honing these little gems. I once heard a senior executive regale a group of rising stars by sharing an experience from thirty years earlier. He actually found himself in an elevator with the head of his department and was impressively prepared for this chance occurrence. The "elevator executive" became his mentor as a result of that short ride, accelerating and directing his career from that point forward.

Sound worth it?

A well-designed pitch is succinct and flexible. I am here to help. Grab a writing utensil and your thinking cap. Here we go.

 ## Take Action!
"Thirty Seconds of Me"

What do you hope to evoke with a successful elevator pitch (which, of course, doesn't have to happen on an elevator)? When and where are you most likely to use your pitch? At work, networking events, business trips, interviews, educational settings? This becomes the anticipated setting for your micro-speech. We use the term *speech* in the loosest possible terms, as it is exceedingly brief and lacks the formality of most speeches.

Most likely situation: _____

_____

Second most likely situation: _____

_____

How will you use your pitch? To find a job, grow your business, identify a mentor, build a professional network, find collaborators?

Primary use: _____

_____

Secondary use: _____

_____

Even seemingly obvious components of your pitch are not. For example, you might think *What is more straightforward than my name?* Take heed! Even how you introduce yourself benefits from forethought. Women are more likely to introduce themselves with just a first name, potentially diminishing their professional presence. Do you prefer to be addressed formally or informally? Do you use your middle name, initials, nickname, or abbreviated version of a longer name?

"What do you do?" The perennial getting-to-know-you question. Again, your response is telling. I might describe myself as a consultant, author, speaker, or coach. A colleague introduces herself as "a business owner," indicating she identifies more with the fact of owning a business than the content of the work product.

What do you do? _____

_____

What do you want to do? _____

_____

What makes you proud? _____

_____

What sets you apart? _____

_____

What inspires you about your work? _____

_____

Enough background work for now. Review what you've written. Put your favorite elements together in a statement of up to six sentences:

_____

_____

_____

_____

_____

_____

These micro-speeches are not intended to say everything there is to know about you. They are teasers or mini-advertisements. A strong pitch leaves your new acquaintance wanting to spend more time conversing with you. This realization frees you from trying to cover the breadth of your career in one fell swoop. Be intriguing, not comprehensive.

From my experience coaching folks on these little gems, many initially lead with a dull opening. Don't bore us to tears! You want pizzazz early on. And maybe a deep pan pizza later. Captivate the listener with what you love about your work, or offer a pithy anecdote. Talking about what revs you up adds oomph. Passion is contagious. The energy uptick is palpable when watching someone recount a pivotal moment versus a recitation of humdrum statistics.

Listeners gather two kinds of information. One is the data: "I was graduated from a prestigious institution with a dream degree. I was promoted five times in two years." Far more compelling is the discovery of your personality. This includes physical presence, sincerity, and attitude. Most listeners are less aware that they're soaking in information through these less overt indicators. Yet these components form the basis for a listener's decision whether to continue the conversation—and the potential relationship.

Practice first in front of a mirror, then with someone whose opinion you value. Time yourself! Hone what works best. If you are up to it, repeat the exercise with a secondary scenario and goal.

 Percolate

Congrats: you scored an interview.

Your hard work pounding the proverbial pavement paid off! You have an interview next Tuesday at 10:00 a.m. Do you:

A. Party by pounding pitchers with the guys.
B. Snooze all weekend in the spirit of being rested.
C. Rally, research, and rehearse.

Sorry to be a buzzkill, but let's celebrate after the job offer. Drinks on me.

Interview Tips

Having done time on the other side of the interview desk, I'm chock-full of ideas.

- Always have an up-to-date resume and bring a hard copy.
- Graduation dates are the closest resumes come to revealing age. Consider removing these, minimizing potential age discrimination.

- Display the utmost respect to those in "mission enabling" roles—receptionists, assistants, cleaning crews, and wait staff. It is good form, shows character, and can open access to guarded pathways.
- Put yourself in the interviewer's shoes. Do your research and emphasize how you specifically add value.
- If meeting in an interviewer's office, take a peek at your surroundings. Desks, walls, and shelves are fodder for conversation and connections.
- Don't ramble! Begin succinctly, pausing to ask if they would like elaboration.

You will almost certainly be asked if you have questions. Prepare inquiries that demonstrate your knowledge about this particular opening. Distinguish yourself from applicants merely pursuing a paycheck. Expand beyond questions on salary and benefits.

Prepare nonwork-related tidbits to share if asked. I heard an extrovert describe introverts as "cagey and not forthcoming." While I took umbrage with the unflattering analysis, introverts do risk appearing aloof unless they plan ahead for "Tell me a little about yourself."

Near the conclusion, ask if you can provide any additional information. As soon as you return home, send a thank-you note.

If you have conducted interviews, reflect on what propelled or prevented an offer. And if you're not selected when applying for a position, it's fair game to follow up with a polite inquiry about what prevented you from getting the job. The response can be worth its weight in gold.

A few interview situations deserve specific attention.

PHONE AND VIDEO INTERVIEWS

Snafus abound. Plan ahead. Be clear on the method of connecting. Who's initiating? Virtual conference? Skype? Cell? Office? Do you have the necessary call-in number? Conference ID? Is the time zone properly calculated? Confirm all details in advance, in writing. Send a calendar notification when the meeting is set and/or an event reminder the day before. Log on early in case of technical difficulties. Situate yourself in a place with strong reception and minimal distractions.

For a video call, dress the part. Adjust the lighting. Face the camera at a good angle. Consider your background!

I've had loads of mishaps in this arena. Let me take the hit for our team.

INTERVIEWS AT RESTAURANTS

You'll likely be invited to a meal-based interview at some point. After fist-bumping your bestie over the free meal ahead, take heed of this clutch advice.

Do your research. An associate was thrilled when he scored a meal with three high-rolling executives. He ordered a Diet Coke. He hadn't bothered to review their website in advance; it prominently featured Pepsi as their lead client. Game over, dude.

Don't get sloppy. Carefully assess address, cross streets, and nearest public transit or parking. I was lined up to meet with an interviewee on East Jefferson, which he conflated with West Jefferson. He arrived thirty minutes late, when I'd already moved on to the next candidate. I wasn't being punitive; I was held to time constraints. Allow extra time for mishaps, and pay attention to details.

Peruse the restaurant website for style of venue and menu. While keeping in mind that online menus can vary from seasonal offerings, plan ahead to mitigate indecision upon arrival. If you have dietary limitations, contact the restaurant in advance to iron out options rather than spending the first moments on site hashing it out with the waitstaff.

Order thoughtfully. Do not select the priciest item. Chose easy-to-eat food. This means no spaghetti or tacos. Avoid items that can get lodged in your teeth. No alcohol or oversized desserts.

Allow the others to order first, attuning your meal to theirs. If no one orders an appetizer, neither do you. If everyone else opts for the breakfast buffet or orders off the lunch specials, consider those options.

This is a professional meeting, not a gathering among friends. Eating is secondary. Unless interviewing to be a sous chef, resist wiping up the sauce with bread or asking for tastes.

Offer to help pay. Casually go for your wallet when the check comes. Most likely they will refuse; do not insist.

INFORMATIONAL INTERVIEWS

Informational interviews are requested to gather data and insights for career advancement or redirection. There is an understanding that this conversation will not directly lead to a job—either there are no openings, or the person requesting the meeting does not yet have the experience or qualifications. Pressing for job opportunities in this context is poor form. Still, it is wise to bring your resume. You can score tips, discover where you have skill gaps, or learn how to proceed in your quest.

Although arranging lunch with a potential mentor might be a top priority for you, it isn't for her. You're not at the top of her to-do list. This is a fact, not a slam.

On the other hand, don't eliminate yourself at strike one by assuming she's too important or too busy. With this in mind, make it easy for your target to say yes. Suggest a meeting that is short, at her convenience, and honors her preferences. Ask what location and timing works best. Entice by suggesting a small selection of happening new restaurants for your meeting.

I regularly receive requests from career changers, job searchers, and students. As in other interview scenarios, keep quality questions in your back pocket; be friendly, not intrusive; dress the part; and follow up with grace and gratitude. Do your homework. If someone wants to "learn about my business" and has not bothered to visit my website or flip through a few of my books, I am not keen on providing a summary for the poorly prepared visitor.

Don't argue! If you are told that earning a PhD is critical in your aspiring career and that's the last thing you want to pursue, lay low. You're allowed to garner second opinions. Refrain from becoming combative or disputing the claim. The advice you least want to hear may become the most important.

Prepare to take notes. In this case a pen and pad are preferable to a tablet or phone, which can be distracting. In a recent meeting with a pair of aspiring entrepreneurs, I offered an array of tips and specific contacts. Neither jotted a single notation.

Be up-front. A colleague asked me to meet with his friend, Edward, confiding that he had been unemployed for several months. I agreed. I arrived prepared to assist Edward in his search, update his resume, and practice interview skills. Unfortunately, Ed was so self-conscious about his professional status that he introduced himself as a gainfully employed consultant. The opportunity was wasted. Unemployment is a tough pill to swallow. However, the majority of us can relate. Looking for a job is perfectly acceptable, not a character flaw. From a successful meeting you might learn of new options, clarify a path forward, discover a mentor, or gain a useful referral.

Notes from the Field
Wake Up and Smell the Coffee

I am frequently solicited for complimentary advice on networking, office politics, being published, what have you. While most meetings blend together over time, a few stand out. An acquaintance asked if we could discuss her upcoming career change. We agreed to meet at a local café during morning rush. She asked about my favorite coffee option, ostensibly to place the order if she arrived first. In fact, she had a scheme. She intentionally arrived early and purchased a high-quality travel mug filled with a latte. I was greeted upon my arrival with this gift and a "Thank you!" I recall her graciousness each time I refill the mug.

I've conducted plenty of interviews for elite graduate and undergraduate programs. Here's the scoop. The universities already have access to your GPA, test scores, and other quantitative qualifications. The interview is to get a sense of your energy, commitment, and personality. You do not need to recite your resume; just casually hand over a hard copy, along with interesting exhibits such as a notable publication, a snippet from a media interview, or an unusual award or accomplishment. Cap it at three; don't go overboard.

Show knowledge of the institution. Demonstrate a targeted interest versus wanting to be admitted somewhere, anywhere. Universities make offers to students most likely to matriculate and thrive. What will be your unique contributions on campus and beyond? I've never recommended admission of a lackluster student with perfect stats. Candidates bursting with enthusiasm for that particular college merit a higher interview rating.

 Pace

Whether on a job hunt or college search, don't feel compelled to attend every networking program within a thirty-mile radius. Try one or two events a month and gauge your effectiveness, inner response, and ability to follow up. Play around with the type, size, and frequency of events to best schedule your time. Fewer, targeted events can yield greater returns.

And in your downtime? I've got the activity for you . . .

Spam, Beautiful Spam

This tip is not particularly zesty. We grudgingly proceed.

Check your spam regularly. Pour a cup of tea or a brewski and open your spam folder. Take a sip and start scrolling. To instill some glamour, envision panning for gold in the wild west. Yes, 99.9 percent of the emails will be—you guessed it—spam! Yet that tenth of a percent could be valuable leads, worth untold millions (give or take a few zeros).

How can you keep your own emails from descending into others' spam? Keep subject lines specific, such as including your name or the person who referred you. Generic proclamations like "A Great Opportunity!" are suspect. Also, misspellings and overly excited punctuation can prompt red flags from spam filters.

 ## Take Action! "Your Job Grid"

Networking can morph into a nebulous, unformulated task. If amoeba impressions are not your thing, try adapting this system to organize your networking efforts. *Your Job Grid* is an insta-structure for growing your infrastructure. How about that?

The grid works as follows. You can enter up to four names in each of the four boxes. *Box A* is for individuals you have met with whom there seems to be mutual interest.

Box B is for those folks who have demonstrated *they* would like an ongoing connection, but *you* are not currently convinced of the benefit or your own interest.

You have a concerted interest in the people of *Box C*, but they do not seem to be aware of you at this point.

Box D is for potential contacts, people you know of through the grapevine or names provided by others. You either have not met them directly or don't know them well enough to know your standing.

Your Job Grid

Me ▶		
Them ▼	I'm Interested	Not Sure
	Box A.	**Box B.**
Demonstrated Interest	1)	1)
	2)	2)
	3)	3)
	4)	4)
	Box C.	**Box D.**
Not on Their Radar	1)	1)
	2)	2)
	3)	3)
	4)	4)

An organized networker can have people in all four boxes at any given time. As you pursue the relationships, placement of each contact within the grid will likely shift.

Caution: Exceeding the numbered spaces provided for active pursuits could entangle you in too many simultaneous loops.

CHAPTER 10

business travel

You leave something of yourself at every meeting with another person.

—Fred Rogers

a. Why does an extrovert join you for dinner on a business trip?

b. Why does an introvert join you for dinner?

Answers:

a. To unwind from a long day by sharing conversation and a meal.

b. To avoid seeming rude.

Let's talk about your next seatmate on a transcontinental flight. "Whoa!" I can hear you shout all the way from here. "I don't want a conversation on an airplane!" And you wonder why you are underconnected.

Take off those noise-canceling headphones! I'm talking to you!

Let's make a deal. You can ignore your seatmates for at least 90 percent of the flight. I ask for about 10 percent of your time. Perfectly reasonable.

I understand not wanting to talk. Travel can deplete energy faster than an outdated cellphone coupled with a cheap charger. Still, I have made stellar contacts on planes and trains, and it was relatively pain-free.

 Prep

A favorite airplane story unfolded when, safely buckled in, I was reviewing my conference evaluations, happily ignoring fellow passengers. My row mate interrupted my reverie, asking, "Are you a consultant?"

Clueless as ever, I replied "How do you know?"

He admitted peeking at my feedback forms, so I handed over the heap, saying, "Take 'em!" Turned out he was a newly minted VP of professional development for the northeast region of a marketing company. He skimmed the evals, took my card, and contacted me the next day to do a training session.

Usually a bit more initiative is required.

You never know who is sitting next to you. I beseech you, learn from my missteps!

Notes from the Field

Introverts, Travel, and Messaging

More business travel means a heightened dependence on electronic means of communication. Do introverts and messaging mix?

An introverted client who claimed to be adamantly antitechnology confessed to loving email. He explained, "It gives me a chance to think over my responses, refine what I say before saying it, and avoid conversing with others when I'm worn out." Having time for processing is a plus. Another introvert confided, "I'm magnetically drawn to the concept of having a conversation without having a conversation."

Extroverts typically prefer instant messaging, which more closely resembles a back-and-forth dialogue. At times, introverts will strategically respond to a text with an email, defusing the expectation of a quick interchange.

As previously explored, typed messaging of all varieties means missing out on nuanced tones and nonverbal cues. I've heard interpretations of written communication that would make your head spin. One client was up in arms because an email concluded with "Thanks" instead of "Thanks!" Another read the affirmation "K..." in a text to mean things weren't okay at all. Don't get me started on the dangers of autocorrect.

Face-to-face interactions are irreplaceable. This is why, despite the option of virtual conferencing, traveling to meet others on site continues to be a valuable business strategy.

Plane and train rides home are ideal opportunities to dash off it-was-lovely-to-meet-you notes with a conversation still fresh in your mind. Driving yourself home, not so much.

As a Cornell MBA student flying from Ithaca, New York, to Manhattan for an Important Job Interview, I was seated next to a stately gray-haired man who was gainfully editing papers. I ignored him, engrossed in reviewing materials on the company flying me out (a novelty for a twenty-six-year-old student). He initiated a conversation. Not interested, I inquired blandly, "What are you working on?" He responded, "Writing a book." Smiling indulgently, I replied, "Well, good luck," and turned back to my reading.

Upon landing, I marched off the airplane and into the taxi shared with four other MBAs from my class (we were not important enough to merit solo fares quite yet). They tumbled in, beside themselves. "We can't believe it! You have all the luck! How come these things happen to you?" I had no idea what they were talking about. Turns out everyone else recognized my seatmate as the dean of Cornell University, a revered academic and respected businessman. Plus, he had a reputation for taking students under his wing. I had completely blown a spectacular opportunity that had been tossed into my lap! The ramifications? Limitless. Not that I'm still harboring regrets. Don't let this happen to you.

The epilogue: I no longer have the faintest clue what company or job I was interviewing for on that trip. I believe I did not receive an offer. The remaining figment of memory, etched permanently, is of me blithely dissing the dean.

Anyone you encounter could transform from a complete stranger into a major player in your life. It happens. Is that possibility worth a few minutes of your time? No need to converse throughout the flight. Be pleasant and casually greet the others in your row as you situate yourself. I bring gum for takeoff and landing and offer row mates a stick. It doesn't matter whether they say yes or no; it is a lovely and appropriate gesture. Other openers, depending on the location of your seat:

- Do you prefer the window shade open or closed?
- Do you want this [newspaper/magazine]?
- Want me to get the light for you?

Then turn back to your work, book, or music. When the drink or snack order is taken, that's round two. Be pleasant, make a remark or two. If they are enthusiastically responding, let it go on for a few minutes, then smile gently and select from the following:

- Unfortunately, I have tons of work to do!
- I'm going to go back to my book now; excuse me.
- I really need a nap before landing.
- It's been nice talking with you!

Be firm and friendly.

From time to time, you will find yourself sincerely wanting the chat to continue—perhaps you believe there is real potential for a continued relationship or sense a spontaneous connection. In either case, as long as you perceive mutual interest, enjoy the conversation.

It's not all smooth sailing. Once, after innocently offering an extrovert my magazine, I was subjected to a play-by-play of his hectic travel and travails over the past four months. After several mind-numbing minutes I mustered an empathetic smile, broke into his blue streak by congratulating him on his tenacity, and moved on to my selection from the previous four all-purpose bullets. He promptly turned to the person across the aisle for a seamless substitution to our conversation.

Relish your I-time; reemerge upon descent. There is limited time remaining to converse, and you can conclude the flight on a friendly note. Offer a card and wish your new connection well. If you definitely want follow-up, request a card as well. Ta-dah! A formula that works. I use it all the time.

Introverts and extroverts have substantially differing sensibilities regarding the protocol for concluding an inflight or rail discourse. If they have engaged in a substantive conversation, introverts are highly likely to conclude with a method to stay in touch. Extroverts are prone to simply say good-bye. An extrovert told me of a time when he and a row mate learned they share a favorite author, launching a lively five-hour discussion. Upon disembarking, they enthusiastically wished each other well, with a cheerful "Have a nice life!" That was that. He considers the encounter a cherished experience.

Opening the door for connection is worth the investment. Heading home from New York City to Washington, DC, by train after a long week, all I truly wanted to do was stare out the window, intermittently playing a word game on my phone. Nevertheless, I followed my own rules and, after plopping myself down, mustered the energy to say hello to my seatmate. He was also returning home after a demanding trip. Within five minutes we discovered a series of remarkable coincidences. Call it serendipity, kismet, or chance. Our lives directly intersected in business, travel, backgrounds, and industry. We've been friends and collaborators ever since.

Percolate

Prioritize scenarios with maximum appeal. While at a four-day conference in Washington, DC, I knew I'd crash and burn if I attended every event. Each evening offered a different theme, and one program was at the National Air and Space Museum. I chose that event because of my inherent interest in the venue. Energized and engaged, I was especially receptive to making new connections.

Take Action!
"Making Conversation"

At your industry conference, you meet an extrovert who immediately begins telling you all about herself. Much of the information is what you would consider personal, yet you realize this is through your subjective introvert lens. Do you:

A. Listen well and ask relevant questions until it is time to part ways?
   or
B. Offer up some of your own personal life, even though it feels awkward?

Both, with a plan. It's tempting to stick with A. However, a one-way relationship is not sustainable or much fun for either party.

Fortunately, in your infinite wisdom, you are reading this book. Together we can prepare you for future encounters with a concrete strategy, mitigating awkwardness. Planning ahead transforms an off-putting situation into a comfortable one.

1. Prepare a list of useful professional facts about yourself.
2. Prepare a list of personal facts you are willing to divulge.

Ensure that your facts have these attributes:

- Short
- Positive
- Versatile
- Easy to explain
- Unique and interesting

To jump-start the process, write examples for the following:

Professional Data

- Current job and workplace . . .

- Professional achievement . . .

- An interesting early or past job . . .

- An inspiring quote . . .

- A professional goal . . .

Personal Tidbits

- Hobbies or interests . . .

_____

- Favorite place . . .

_____

- A memorable vacation . . .

_____

- A family fact . . .

_____

- A personal goal . . .

_____

Test-driving responses aloud with a trusted colleague, friend, or family member commits your options to memory, making them quickly accessible when caught in the moment. Your listener can help you weave these comments seamlessly into a conversation—preventing disjointed non sequiturs. Some can be adapted into openers:

"My daughter would love this place!"

"This is quite different from Boston."

"I took a great walk outside this evening—perfect weather."

"I've started my own garden and aspire to grow peppers like these."

"This program is well done. Running a conference is tough!"

Carefully worded questions also open the door for further conversation. As a general rule, start with open, nonpersonal questions, allowing new acquaintances to decide how specific or personal a response to give.

"What do you know about the keynote speaker tomorrow?"

"Do you live far from here?"

"When did you arrive?"

"Do you have any tips about things to do here?"

"How long have you worked in this field?"

"Have you been to this conference before?"

. . . the list goes on. Practice makes inventing new questions easier. Make comments affirming, not an opportunity to complain. Critical remarks get tossed around with astonishing regularity and reveal a lot about a personality.

- This isn't a very inspired food selection.
- Couldn't they have provided group transportation?
- These nametags sure don't stay on well.
- Seems like they skimped this year.
- I hate these events.
- Isn't the speaker ever going to stop talking?
- I can't stand this city.
- What terrible weather!
- I'm exhausted.
- Look at these drink lines.
- This hotel has gone downhill.

I have heard all of the above and then some at networking events. The list could fill a book. Not a particularly inspiring book, but lengthy. Do you want to hang out with the people who made these comments? Me neither. Don't be one of them. Above all, restrain yourself from making negative comments about others. It's never worth the witty quip. The inevitable result: those listening will assume you'll talk about them as well.

I do not recommend initiating a question about a new acquaintance's home life. Family is a touchy topic for many and can lead to an awkward interaction. However, casually mentioning your own family can open the door for connectivity when appropriate.

Saying, for example, "My daughter would love this place" allows for responses such as:

- How old is she?
- Do you have a photo with you?
- I have a daughter, too . . .
- I have young sons, and they would wreck the place!

Each provides different platforms for connection. A well-thought-out small-talk strategy can read as seamlessly off-the-cuff.

 Pace

For extroverts, mingling is a relaxing, rewarding aspect of work. For introverts, expectations to socialize amid jam-packed agendas can drain you drier than the Sahara.

I was tickled when at a convention I was caught in the path of an introvert cruising away from a group of attendees who were merging to engage in conversation. Whizzing past, he tossed me a throwaway line: "I don't want to get caught in that vortex!" Hilariously, an extrovert's friendly discourse is an introvert's vortex!

SAY NO

Remember the last time you wound up trapped in the matrix of a three-hour, two-dozen-person business dinner? The small talk drained you, and the food was drenched in an unidentified sauce. Let's ensure that next time you kick this energy drain to the curb.

Keep it short. Repeat after me: "Thanks, but I am going to take it easy tonight." No elaborate explanation or apology is required. Details allow others to poke holes in your reasoning. For example:

| "I need my sleep." | → | "You can sleep on the airplane tomorrow!" or |
| | ← | "I am sure we will be back by 10!" |

This digresses into an avoidable argument. Take a look at two sample dialogues. Notice how good intentions devolve into peer pressure and guilt trips. The extrovert remains consistent; the introvert's responses change.

BAD

E: Hey, you're joining us tonight, right? Everyone is meeting in the lobby at 6:30 p.m.

I: Ummmm . . . [hasn't prepared a response, trying to drum one up at the last minute]

E: Great! It's going to be a blast—first drinks, then dinner at a terrific steakhouse.

I: Ahhhh, actually, I'm kinda wiped out from today.

E: You have over an hour to rest up! Let's meet at the bar at 6:00, before the others.

I: Well, maybe.

E: Don't be a deadbeat! Everyone is going.

I: I think I'm going to take it easy tonight.

E: But you said yes. We never see you out. People will start to talk!

I: Okay. [dreading the night and kicking himself]

GOOD

E: Hey, you're joining us tonight, right? Everyone is meeting in the lobby at 6:30 p.m.

I: I don't think so.

E: Don't be a deadbeat! Everyone is going. Come on, it'll be fun!

I: Thanks; I'm going to take it easy tonight.

E: What?? We never see you out. People will start to talk—ha-ha!

I: I'm staying in. Have fun. See you tomorrow!

Smile, wave, and hightail it to the elevator bank.

Remind yourself that it's great that extroverts are making the most of their trip. You are also making the most of *your* trip.

How protective you are of your I-time depends on your energy level and placement on the introvert continuum. A strong introvert running on reserves requires more solo time to recharge. A slight introvert with stored energy may decide to join the others initially, then turn in early. In either case, prepare your exit strategy and depart guilt-free.

Take Action!
"As If"

Welcome to the world of *as if reframes*. Glad you'll join me on this tour of new and improved reality interpretations. Here's how it works. Write down one of your operating beliefs. Virtually anything works. If you have no idea what I'm talking about, consider a networking-related impression that you believe is true. Write what comes to mind. If you are feeling noncommittal, here are some examples:

- I can't network.
- People don't like me.
- If I act friendly I won't be authentic.
- I am not capable of being more assertive.
- Sheila is not interested in what I have to say.

What if you behaved *as if* your belief weren't true? This has nothing to do with objective reality. (Which does not really exist. Let's cover that in my next book.) The *as if* frame challenges you to live *as if* something different, even the precise opposite, were true. This exercise requires a leap of faith or, for you logical folks, a suspension of disbelief. This isn't about certainty or empirical facts. The point is rewiring your brain for heightened success, not winning a debate tournament. Remind me to dig out my high school debate team trophy collection.

For kicks, let us practice by replacing the preceding list of beliefs with contrary options. Choose your favorites from the upcoming selections. How would life change if you behaved *as if* the following were true? Notice how it's possible to play around with various types of reframes.

- I can network.
- People like me.
- I can be friendly and true to myself.
- I can be more assertive in meeting people.
- I am interested in what Sheila has to say.
- Sheila is interested in what I have to say.
- I am interested in what I have to say.

Want another application of this little tool? Think back to the last time you went to a social or professional event and got stuck for a period of time talking to the *wrong person*. I think you know what I mean. Someone you instantly determined, with your infallible spidey sense, was the least interesting person in the room. You may protest that you do not think of others so callously. Even if you did not have such a harsh thought, the following inner monologue excerpt may ring a bell:

Why did I bother coming out tonight? Now I am stuck talking to this stick-in-the-mud. I mean, really. How annoying. I got cornered, and this is turning into a complete waste of time. (Yawn.) Maybe if I look around the room enough, he will pick up on my cues and move on. Not with my luck. How can I get the heck out of here?

What if you were to pretend, for a trial period of three months, that everyone is the *right person*—even if only for the length of time of that particular encounter? What do you imagine would happen? I will make an educated guess.

When you choose to believe the person in front of you is supposed to be there at this moment, guess what? Due to your innovative approach to meeting people, you treat her like the right person. Even temporarily, she becomes the right person. You become more animated, less distracted, more interested, and more interesting yourself, opening new opportunities for you both.

I am pretty good at reading people yet am regularly wrong about who will eventually become the right people in my life. I like that I am wrong—that I cannot always distinguish who will have a featured role in my life story and who will be fast forgotten.

Behave *as if* everyone is the right person. There are infinite variations on *as if* frames. While you can practice this tool anywhere, on the road is a fine time to test-drive reframes.

CHAPTER 11

structuring events that work for all

You can make more friends in two months by becoming interested in other people

than you can in three years by trying to get other people interested in you.

—Dale Carnegie

No Event Is a Good Event Quiz

True or False

For people who hate networking, casual chatting is better than structured activities.

Answer:

False

You may have unpleasant memories of standing at an event, a wilting networking wallflower, wistfully watching extroverts swirl around the room collecting people, business cards, and toothpicks from those tasty hors d'oeuvre platters. Perhaps this observation convinced you of your own inadequacy: *I don't want to talk to these people, and they don't want to talk to me. I'm outta here.*

Stop the cycle!

Fast-forward, and now you're in charge, running an event to call your own. Well, maybe someone else gets the credit and is thanked from the podium on the big night, but we both know it was all your doing. Or it is not officially a networking event, but, as we've agreed, many interactions by other names have networking potential. How do you create an event inclusive for a range of temperaments? How can you run programs sensitive to diverse styles?

Start at the beginning.

Prep

Stop and think. When planning an event, do you kick off with a brainstorming session? Many do. Your committee might brainstorm ideas for venue, theme, scope, and other programmatic components. Yet most brainstorming sessions are inherently extro-centric.

Someone poses a topic, standing at attention in front of the group armed with a semi-dried-out marker and seen-better-days whiteboard. Suggestions are solicited. Some participants call out ideas, dutifully transcribed for all to see. Others say nothing. To the novice observer, those actively sharing ideas are invested in the process, whereas the quiet attendees are (select one): disinterested, dull, daft, distracted, or desultory. And those are just the d's.

What's really going on? The very process is designed for people who talk to think. Because introverts think to talk, by the time they deem their contributions well formed enough to speak aloud, the fast-moving process has progressed to the next phases of analyzing, followed by ranking. A notable exception is that introverts speak up—quickly and at length—when a specific topic of significant import is broached.

Luckily, there is an easy fix to the terrible injustice done to free-associating introverts the world over. Next time you run a brainstorming session, distribute pens and paper. Announce the topic. Ask participants to reflect and contemplate potential solutions, inviting them to jot down their musings. Providing even a single minute is peachy. Introverts aren't slow, just thoughtful.

Keep track of time; do not trust yourself to guess when the minute is up. Next, invite people to call out ideas and/or pass forward their written ideas, which you can read aloud and add to the visible list. Prepare to be surprised by how many more ideas you get from the entire group.

At the other end of the spectrum, how can extroverts ensure not oversharing in a brainstorming session—or a meeting of any kind? An extrovert taught me an acronym with wallop. WAIT stands for "Why Am I Talking?" He said asking himself this pertinent question at regular intervals has improved the quality and quantity of his input.

Early in the process of event preparation, take time to identify the hidden resources of those around you. Learn about others' interests, backgrounds, and skills. A survey will increase the depth of response from introverts. Freely share information about the event, opening the door to a wide range of input. By doing so, you can avoid situations like this one:

One of my nonprofit clients ran a major event highlighting the customs of a distant culture. Afterward, the event planner learned that the spouse of a colleague in accounting was from that region. He would have been a wonderful resource, except no one had thought to share information prior to the event with those in seemingly unrelated departments.

ASSUME NOTHING

What's the best way to integrate introverts, centroverts, and extroverts at your programs? Many times, I've seen the surprising reality unfold.

Introverts insist they do not want to be coerced into interactions. Personalities across the spectrum profess to dislike coordinated efforts to engage with unknown others. Don't believe them! I am here to tell you that virtually anyone can absolutely benefit from well-facilitated activities. Mixing up participants and providing conversational prompts is doing everybody a big favor.

Ultimately, those who grumble the most about structured meet-and-greets benefit the most.

 Percolate

A networking event that works for all will flow seamlessly between structure and elasticity. If it is a recurring program, consider designating those new to the event with a symbol on their nametags, encouraging long-timers to reach out.

The activities offered here as samples are easy to implement and have broad applications. Embellish, customize, and adapt to taste. One or two per event is ample.

Place Cards

My riff on typical folded-card name tents works at meetings and confer-ences from thirty to three hundred participants during a group meal. Make small table tents with creative characteristics and descriptors, and put one at each place setting, facing out (*speaks 3+ languages, plays golf, has a PhD, knows how to juggle, loves to cook, avid reader . . .*). Have extras and blanks on hand. As participants enter, invite them to sit at a place with a table tent that describes them.

This setup serves a dual purpose. Participants sit with a fusion of col-leagues, and each place card is a mini-conversation starter—providing topics to discuss. If a few people cannot find a match, they can pick from the extras or write their own.

Nametag Art

Provide pens in a range of colors next to nametags on a table near the entrance. As people arrive, ask them to draw on their nametags a small picture that symbolizes something about themselves. As participants circulate, these symbols provide a starting point for mingling, offering greater insight into others than basic introductory conversations. Yes, I have tried this with "serious" groups, and they loved the results.

Action Bingo

A bit of up-front work and creativity pays off with this bingo adap-tation. Create several different versions of bingo boards—make each board with five boxes across and four down for a total of twenty squares. I make about ten versions per event, but four or five is fine. Write a different attribute, hobby, or trait in each box (*gardener, class cutup, love the snow, never tired, born to ride*—a range of specifics, generalities, and metaphors). Print enough copies to give one board to each person. Provide five minutes to play.

Participants find someone with one of the traits on their board and get that person to sign in the box. Participants cannot sign their own board and can solicit one signature per person. You can give a small prize to the winner(s)—whoever has the most spaces filled.

This infuses the room with energy in a short period of time, facilitates new connections, and encourages continued discussion through the information learned. I like enriching the debrief to include discussion of how goals impact behaviors in the exercise and how initial perceptions of others may mislead.

Musical Greet

At the start of a meet-and-greet program, get everyone's attention for a brief activity. Tell them you are going to play music (about fifteen seconds per interlude) while they stroll around. When the music stops, ask participants to find someone they don't know nearby and provide them with a topic such as *first job, memorable vacation, dream meal,* and the like. Tell them they get one minute to share responses. Play music again while they meander around to mix themselves up for the next round. Announce a different conversation starter for each pairing. Repeat for five rounds. Sample topics include:

- What was your first job?
- Describe your dream meal.
- Demonstrate or reveal a hidden talent.
- Where did you go on a memorable vacation?
- Tell about something you won.
- What are you most proud of this past year?

People light up, sharing heartfelt stories and positive memories. Plus, in under ten minutes, everyone has met five new people!

Learn Names

The most beautiful word is your own name. Particularly if it's Italian.

A client explained his impression of a senior colleague: "He is a really good guy"—reflecting with a laugh—"or maybe it is because he always remembers my name." Learning and using names is a surefire method to create rapport. Too bad we're so lousy at it. Most extroverts *and* introverts get a failing grade in *The Basics of Name Recollection*. Take my tips, please.

1. First, you have to care. Give the person introducing herself your complete focus. Be honest. Many people cannot repeat a name even moments after hearing it. Pay attention to the person in front of you. This also means filtering out competing stimuli.
2. When first introduced, look directly at the other person's eyes.
3. Repeat the other person's name up to three times during your first conversation. More is too much.
4. Associate the name with another person you know.
5. Ask the origin or spelling.

Taking it to the next level, tap into your primary processing system. If you are unsure, experiment with the following three to discover what techniques work best for you.

Auditory	Visual	Kinesthetic
■ Ask the spelling, repeating for confirmation.	■ See the name in color or written out.	■ Imagine the person engaged in an activity, particularly one featuring alliteration (Rick raking, Cathy cooking).
■ Clarify the pronunciation.	■ Make a visual image of the name.	■ Notice the person's stance and demeanor.
■ Connect the name to his or her voice.	■ Look at the nametag.	■ Write down the name soon after talking.
■ Recall a song with the name, if possible.	■ Link the name to the person's appearance.	■ If seated in a group, draw a chart with the names.
■ Say the name lyrically in your head.	■ Envision a person you know with the same name.	■ Draw the letters with your finger through the air—after moving away!

Do Your Part

Assisting others in recollecting your name is a corollary to learning theirs. Strategies vary depending on how familiar your name is to the local population.

Everyone	Well-Known Names	Less-Recognized Names
■ Wear a nametag.	■ Ask whether they know another [your name].	■ Spell your name slowly.
■ Ensure that your nametag is visible when sitting down.	■ Clarify your name's spelling.	■ Offer a rhyme or memory tool.
■ Reiterate your name.	■ Recall someone well-known with the same name.	■ Reintroduce yourself the first few times you meet.

I was facilitating a communication styles program for highly skilled engineers. Mandatory attendance was decreed from above. The sponsoring executive suggested we entitle it "The 'Show Up or Be Fired' Seminar!"—a suggestion that I tactfully sidestepped.

Nearly all the attendees typed out, using this book's assessment tool, as introverts. Observable class participation was low. We flew through the agenda. I suspected this behavior was not indicative of disinterest. Introverts require time to process, and the attendees' nonverbal cues indicated full engagement in the course content. Even before seeing their results, my hunch was confirmed at the first break. I was encircled by students asking one-on-one questions. Virtually all participant questions were posed between sessions.

Cognitive Dissonance

Allow me to refresh your memory of that freshman Psych 101 class you took in your misguided youth for an easy A. *Cognitive dissonance* ring a bell, anyone? This psychological phenomenon captures the human condition of wanting to be right. Imagine I have a theory. I become attached to my hypothesis. If evidence in the outside world contradicts my hypothesis, my brain kicks into high gear to disprove the data and cling to my theory. Brains steadfastly gather and accumulate data to support our beliefs, sorting out, ignoring, and disproving contradictory evidence.

Let's drive this home. Think of the population subgroup that you secretly believe are the worst drivers out there. Don't tell me! I don't want my own theory clouded by yours. Imagine you are driving on the highway and in a hurry. You are in the left lane in a 55-mph zone. You assess how fast you can go without being pulled over. As you cruise along at 64 mph, you approach a car directly in front of you, plodding along at an inconceivably rude 50 mph. In the fast lane! You swing into the right lane to pass and can't resist a peek into the other car to

Notes from the Field
Calibration

Coming home from a business trip, I took a connecting flight that became a delayed layover in Oklahoma City. After two hours of waiting, hearing continually pushed-back flight status reports, it was nearing 10:00 p.m. Finally, we were told our flight was canceled. This tardy announcement was bad news, as there would be no way out until morning. A lengthy line of disgruntled and exhausted would-be passengers wove through an otherwise deserted airport terminal.

No one was happy.

In bounded a terrifyingly perky customer service representative, all smiles. Her demeanor was a perfect fit for Disney's Main Street parade.

Except we were a long, long way from Disney World. Her mood was so hopelessly incongruent with the customer base that even the meekest in the crowd became nearly ballistic. How dare she be in a good mood when our night was ruined. Ruined!

Calibration means syncing tone and attuning yourself to others' state of mind. The idea is to meet people where they are. This does not mean yelling and screaming to show your support for someone else who is upset. On the other hand, an overly relaxed response can be taken as a lack of interest, or even mockery. Acknowledge that you understand why the situation would make someone upset. A display of empathy does not imply that you would react the same way. You are merely validating, rather than discarding, the other person's emotional response.

Positive moods can be contagious. *Most* of the time. Matching the prevalent energy of a group is equally important. If you're leaving a session on the dire consequences of unchecked global warming, restrain yourself from commenting brightly on what a delightful, unexpectedly balmy day it is for January.

When aiming to build connections, notice speech patterns, volume, and body language. Practice modifications of your baseline style for maximum flexibility.

As for me, I have been accused of being a bit of a loudmouth (another introvert stereotype bites the dust!). Yet I take it down a notch when meeting with a soft-spoken client. With my personality intact, I fine-tune my outward expression for purposes of rapport.

---

check your personal bad driver theory. Aha! It *is* one of them! You *knew* it! You enjoy a smidgen of self-satisfaction that you were right.

Now, take the same scenario, except that when passing, you peek at the driver and it is *not* one of them. In fact, this driver looks very similar to you. Do you trash your theory? Do you think, *Well, that was a good lesson in human nature: I was wrong*? No. You shrug and think,

Hmpf, that's strange. And you go on your way. It was a nonevent. Data discarded.

Event planners frequently make assumptions about what will or won't resonate with participants—and sort for data that supports their hypothesis. Raising your awareness of the limitations and pitfalls of cognitive dissonance enables you to expand your receptiveness to new and different ideas.

Building rapport with attendees is key to pulling off successful events, so sync communications to complement—not clash, as in this illustration of failed calibration.

Finally, when creating events, keep circling back to what resonates with diverse styles.

REFRESHER COURSE

High-performance introverts shine in:

- One-on-one discussion
- In depth knowledge and expertise
- Thoughtful Reflection

Introvert strengths include:

- Focusing attention
- Listening deeply
- Following up

High-performance centroverts shine in:

- Coalitions with diverse members
- Facilitation
- Mediation

Centrovert Strengths include:

- Bridging divides
- Developing buy-in
- Enabling connections

High-performance extroverts shine in:

- Group discussion
- Outreach Effects
- Interaction on a range of topics

Extrovert strengths include:

- Promoting projects and people
- Expanding team networks
- Creating excitement for new ideas

CHAPTER TWELVE

follow up or go home

"One of the most powerful networking tools is to provide immediate value . . .

the moment you identify a way to help someone, take action."

—Lewis Howes

Quiz

A conversation reveals potential for a symbiotic connection. Contact info is exchanged. Who is predisposed to follow up?

Answer:

Those who perceive themselves as underconnected are the most likely to follow up and create relationships with depth.

You attend an event and engage in the most revered, all-star networking behaviors. You are friendly and witty. You consume only food that can't get stuck between your teeth. Your dazzling, off-the-cuff remarks flow forth, as a small crowd gazes on in awe. You propel yourself out of the room, waving at new acquaintances—neither overstaying your welcome nor rushing out suspiciously early. Watching the cityscape dreamily rush by from the backseat of your Lyft, you relive the evening with a self-satisfied smile.

The next day—and the next and the next—your hectic routine of work, home, and sundry demands lassos your life. A few weeks later, you discover an unceremonious heap of tattered business cards at the bottom of your briefcase. A perfunctory skim leaves you with the vaguest recollection of where they might have originated. Feeling efficient, you toss the whole pile in the trash.

Stop the presses! Your efforts don't amount to a hill of beans if you're not following up. Without follow-up, you're just talking to people. Even if you implement all the other tips in this book, I won't give you a high five. Commit this admonishment to memory:

If you're not following up, you're not networking!

Pure and simple.

Why don't people follow up? Let's debunk five popular excuses.

Flimsy Excuse #1:

"I forget names and faces. I have a bad memory!"

Stalwart Response #1:

Guess what? So do I! An A+ memory is not a prerequisite for follow-up. Quality systems save the day. After an encounter worthy of next steps, here's your plan. Offer your business card and request one in return. Immediately upon parting, note pertinent information on the front of the card you received, such as:

- Name, with correct pronunciation hints
- Event location and date
- Topics discussed (upcoming project, recent travel, interests)
- Intended follow-up ideas

No more kvetching about your ever-weakening memory.

Flimsy Excuse #2:

"I sent a general follow-up to everyone I met at that thing."

Stalwart Response #2:

That's supremely sloppy. You're better than that! Any lazy bum can send a generic follow-up to a bcc'd list of recent encounters. This is a hazy imitation of real follow-up. Don't bother. Nonspecific language masking as a personal note is quickly dismissed. Best case, your insincere emails go right into the trash bin. Worst case, you get a reputation as a phony. Lucky for you, a genuine note outperforms impersonal gibberish. Read on.

Flimsy Excuse #3:

"I'm too busy."

Stalwart Response #3:

You needn't stay in touch with every person you meet. Quality over quantity. Choose where to direct your effort and accomplish meaningful follow-up with remarkable alacrity. Still, don't conflate being selective with being lackadaisical. Prioritizing means putting more effort into fewer people. Rather than spending two hours sending vague emails to everyone you met at a three-day conference, focus on the handful that made the strongest impression. A fraction of your time, a higher return on investment.

Flimsy Excuse #4:

"They can contact me if interested! Following up seems needy or pushy or desperate" (take your pick).

Stalwart Response #4:
That's ridiculous. How could you say such a thing?

What you're really doing is putting the onus on others—a surefire way to lose valuable contacts. It's all in the execution. Polite, sincere follow-up does not come across as needy or pushy. Or, for that matter, desperate. Have you been a recipient of follow-up that rubbed you the wrong way? Reflect on why it had that impact. Was it aggressive, pleading, or demanding? Ensure that yours is respectful, articulate, and thoughtful.

Flimsy Excuse #5:

"I followed up and didn't hear back!"

Stalwart Response #5:
Sorry, Charlie. Follow-up is rarely a one-off. You may not hear back initially for loads of reasons, and virtually none of these are intended as a personal affront. More on this ahead.

 Prep

Be in a positive state of mind. If you find yourself falling back on a flimsy excuse, it's time to revisit your self-talk (chapter 4). Convincing yourself that others have little interest in you is often pure projection.

Lack of response ≠ lack of interest.

Be Resilient

Let's not mince words. People are stressed, overwhelmed, and—behind their shiny veneer—alarmingly disorganized. That means diligent outreach can wind up lost in space at the other end. When our efforts don't get a chipper reply within a few days, all kinds of reasons come to mind. *My follow-up was stupid! He can't stand me! She never wants to see me again! I blew it!*

Far more likely? They never read it, read it and got distracted, intended to reply, could swear they did reply, or are dealing with their own variety of crises. Want to hear my own examples?

1. I pitched a clever, yet offbeat idea and figured that not hearing back was evidence that the recipient was fundamentally offended by my concept. I kicked myself for having the audacity to suggest it. The next week she gave notice at her firm. I realized that while my little idea was foremost in my mind, it was inconsequential in her whirlwind of changing jobs. She forwarded my concept to her replacement.

2. I had a positive relationship with a new client, and she was pleased with our work together. It seemed a sure thing that we'd collaborate again. On and off over several months I sent messages and emails casually checking in, reminding her of upcoming projects she had suggested. She didn't respond. A full year later, I tried again. This time she responded immediately and enthusiastically. She had been dealing with back-to-back family and work issues and now wanted to arrange a call ASAP. She showed no indication of ever noticing my previous emails, which I deemed best unmentioned.

3. I got a lead and sent materials upon request. We scheduled meetings three times; he canceled each last minute. I nearly gave up, let time pass, and finally checked in one last time. He thanked me sincerely for staying in touch. Turned out he had undergone two surgeries in that timeframe and was now ready to roll.

I have more examples of this nature than I can count. Of course, math was never my strong suit.

Sometimes all you hear are crickets on the other end of the proverbial phone line. Rather than jumping on the crowded bandwagon of self-effacement, remind yourself that there's lots more going on in others' lives than you can imagine.

Takeaways:
- Be kind to yourself; it is doubtful that you blew it.
- Be patient with others.
- Don't burn bridges.
- All's well that ends well.

Don't bother pointing out the time-consuming proposal that was demanded ASAP, then promptly ignored. Resist punitive jabs such as, "As I already said in my first email . . ." That's a fast track to nowhere. Plus, the written word is easily misconstrued.

 Percolate

How does a lead flow into results?

In your initial encounter, assess what matters to your new contact and let that guide you. Is there a sense of urgency? Are they merely fact finding? Do they prioritize relationship building? Calibrate your communication to these cues. If you're not sure, ask questions.

When checking in, be upbeat and concise. Heed your instincts.

Timing. Follow up within two days, with the interaction fresh in your minds. We forget half of what we hear within about forty-eight hours. Memories and inspiration fade fast.

One caveat. Monday is generally the worst day to follow up, make requests, or ask for any kind of favor. You might be familiar with the Monday morning feeling of dread stemming from hefty piles of mail, messages, demands, and deadlines. Nine-to-fivers are unlikely to respond to anything perceived as nonurgent on the first day of a workweek.

There are exceptions, and I happen to be one. Inexplicably, I tend to be gung-ho on Mondays, eager to whiz through a bunch of to-dos. To make matters worse, I'm a morning person. Unless I keep myself in check, I'm inclined to start leaving messages prior to 9:00 a.m. local time. If you share this propensity, resist! I consciously postpone non-pressing follow-up until Tuesday. In fact, I'm writing these very words on a Monday morning, redirecting my attention. Tuesdays have a better track record for responsiveness, and Fridays are even better. As the most laid-back weekday, Fridays are a prime time for follow-up and even asking for raises!

Personalize. Introverts appreciate the written word, so crafting a tailored note for a new contact is a perfect fit. To merit a networking gold star, reference a topic from the initial encounter. Ask about the new project or how coaching Jake's soccer team went. You will make a smashing second impression.

Retro alert! For maximum pizzazz, send a letter via actual mail. This gesture gets noticed. While not necessary for run-of-the-mill correspondence, handwritten notes pack a punch when you want to stand out from the crowd. Keep a supply of stamps and classy cards, and you'll find writing a note takes no more time than emailing. Oh, and be legible. If that's beyond your bailiwick, printing out and signing a typed letter is the backup plan.

As in all aspects of networking, let the real you shine through. One caution for baby boomers: times have changed. Unless specifically requested, resist following up via a phone call. Unscheduled professional calls tend to catch people off guard nowadays.

Be useful. To cement an initial connection, consider sending your new acquaintance a relevant link, reference, or article of interest. A thoughtful gesture conveys that you recall the conversation and are useful to boot. Include your website address so the recipient can easily learn more about what you have to offer.

If there is no deadline-driven need, it's fine to let some time pass before a second message. Better to wait two weeks than bombard with emails twice a week.

Submissions. What about a time-sensitive matter? When providing a proposal, job application, statement of work, project quote, or the like, it is perfectly acceptable to request acknowledgment of receipt with your initial submission.

If you hear nothing back with the deadline approaching, email a brief check-in that includes the original submission. Keep it short and simple:

"Just confirming you received my proposal sent June 18, attached here. Let me know if I can provide additional information at this time."

The Squeaky Wheel

Does the squeaky wheel get the grease? Or does it make you greasy? How much is too much? What counts as squeaky, anyway? So confusing!

Too much follow-up can make you persona non grata. On the other hand, vanishing without a trace makes you impossible to find even when sought out.

You want to stay on people's radar. I've tried in vain to track down preferred vendors for repeat business. Friendly updates and notifications once or twice a year do your customers a service. Provide a method to "unsubscribe" to keep your reminders welcome.

Recall a time when a vendor reached out at the most opportune time, gently reminding you to reorder supplies, schedule a training, or get an oil change. The product or service was the last thing on your mind—until you found yourself signing up. You can increase the likelihood of making this happen for *your* contacts by keeping track of when a customer is most likely to need a service based on previous conversations ("We schedule our trainings in April"), knowledge of their business (spending more at the end of the fiscal year) or tracking typical product cycles.

I love when clients exclaim, "You read my mind!" when I reach out at precisely the right time. What's really going on is that I am being attentive and organized.

At the same time, don't be a pest. Following up too fervently places you midway between annoying and desperate on the "people to avoid" spectrum. It also raises the question of why you have so much time on your hands.

 ## Pace

Who's important? That's the big question. My exasperating response? "You never know!"

Have you ever hit it off with someone for no apparent reason? Despite clicking, you may assess that this person couldn't possibly contribute to your current endeavors. He is new to the field. She is on a different career trajectory. He recently retired. She is based overseas.

Maintain that connection! Don't second guess or create an elaborate algorithm. Stay in touch, withholding expectations of where it might lead. This inexplicable link might result in a surprising networking bridge down the road.

Authenticity is a stronger foundation for positive outcomes than working a contact with the explicit purpose of getting ahead.

Irrespective of your genius-level IQ, you're no psychic when it comes to where a relationship might lead. I maintained a friendship with a colleague long after he retired, occasionally catching up over coffee or a walk.

Fast-forward a few years. I get a seemingly random phone call from a Fortune 500 company interested in working with me. At the end of the conversation, the HR director casually mentions she'd heard of me from that friend's wife, who now works there.

Outside the Box

You've hung in this far, so I'll share my most ridiculous touching-base strategy. While I once vowed to never fess up to my harebrained scheme, time makes fools of us all. I had time on my hands and wanted a reason to remind contacts of my existence. Mid-March and time to get creative. St. Patrick's Day, anyone?

I decided to send my contacts named Patricia, Patrick, and Pat special greetings on behalf of "their" holiday. You don't need a heck of a lot of hits. Out of twenty messages sent, five politely thanked me. One responded enthusiastically, saying it had been too long and "Will you join me for lunch?"—igniting five years of lively business together.

You may question my enthusiasm, wondering *Five years; what's the big deal? Compared to the reign of the triceratops, that's nothing.* If you mention the Cretaceous period in the same complaint, I'll be duly impressed. Okay, maybe five years isn't *super* long, but the quality of our collaboration was memorable and rewarding.

Consider the climates, holidays, or interests of regions where you do business. Wish your Canadian counterparts a happy Flag Day in February. Send a virtual toast to British clients celebrating a royal wedding. Congratulate your Japanese offices for winning an Olympic medal. Impress Aussies by commenting on a regional election down under.

Letting Go

You've made a goodwill gesture. You're on the board of a professional association and offer your new contact a complimentary six-month membership or free admission to an upcoming program. She declines, which you interpret to mean that she is self-conscious about accepting. You double down, insisting it is your pleasure, letting her know how much she would benefit.

Although difficult to comprehend, she may not want to join, attend, or meet. A marvelous opportunity to you might be a time drain to her. This is a no-judgment zone.

Inexplicable preferences do not betray faulty wiring.

Make the offer, send a gentle reminder, and accept a no by saying the door is open if she changes her mind.

Some people are self-proclaimed joiners; others need to pare down commitments. What if you're in the latter group? Saying no is uncomfortable. You don't want to seem ungrateful. Or, worse, unhelpful. You've never been on the Office Family Fun Day committee. Maybe you're not the parent-teacher organization type. Perhaps grassroots triggers your hay fever.

You're good as you are. Stand firm on your outer limits; no need to compare. If you sense that another obligation might push you over the edge, honor that instinct. No one wins when a guilt-ridden, haphazard, and ill-conceived can-do attitude morphs into a panic attack.

Try this on for size: "While I appreciate your reaching out, no thank you."

No need to elaborate. Explanations and excuses unnecessarily entangle, sparking rebuttals such as:

- It's a mere few meetings!
- You're perfect for the role.
- We always have fun!
- This is a very minor obligation.

Just reply, "I promised myself I wouldn't take on any more commitments at this point." That line alone is worth this book's cover price. I repeat: *Do not elaborate.*

Despite best efforts, some sought-after connections don't pan out. You may never know the full story. At a certain point, outreach yields diminishing marginal returns, and it's time to move on. In some programs, I tap participants to convince others, who don't like a particular food, to taste it anyway. They try out an array of tactics and are often remarkably successful. Occasionally the "convincers" face a "resistor" who is actually allergic to the food of choice. In this case, expending more energy is not correlated with better results. Don't obsess over sunk costs. Knowing when to cut your losses is as important as being attuned to genuine receptivity.

CHAPTER 13

creating a community

Yesterday I was clever, I wanted to change the world.

Today I am wise, I'm changing myself.

—Rumi

Birthday Quiz

What is the worst part of having a birthday?

Answer:

For extroverts, fretting about whether enough
people will show up to celebrate

For introverts, fretting about all the people
that will want to talk to you*

---

*Shout-out to Sapling Press, from whom this insight is adapted.

Social Networking

Virtual exchanges have somehow appropriated the descriptor *social networking*. A rather inapt description; there is nothing traditionally social about communicating *en masse* with large numbers of widely scattered people. In my estimation, actually being present deserves that distinction.

There are indisputable benefits to technological advances, including the enablement of remote connections. Even so, being together in person is inimitable. Which brings us to enriching and expanding your localized in-person social networks. If you're interested in ways to meet and socialize with real human beings, we're on the same page.

Pace

You moved to a new city? Or perhaps you are hankering for friends who share your interests. Do you and a partner want to expand your social circles? Maybe you enrolled in a full-time post-graduate program. Possibly you've had a life change and are making a fresh start. Looking to benefit from networking beyond your work life? If so, you'll benefit from a leisurely stroll through this chapter.

Professional networking, in general terms, has the aim of furthering your career. Personal networking has different objectives, yet honoring your natural preference remains central to success. You are who you are. Your score on chapter 2's self-assessment drives your version of creating new connections. A preference for one-on-one conversations and a need for processing time, for example, influence the approach that works best for you.

At times, personal and professional spheres overlap. Friendship may lead to business, and business may lead to friendship. While socializing can result in professional advancement, this is a potential side effect, not a goal. To retain others' good graces, keep this distinction crystal clear.

Do not be That Person who ceaselessly self-markets while out and about on evenings, weekends, and holidays. You know who I'm talking about. The one who, at a casual brunch for friends, hands out brochures on his latest in a string of startups. Or lobbies for investors by cornering revelers at the neighborhood holiday party. This is not a path to prosperous business; it is a path to losing friends.

Keep intentions clean. A friend invited me to hang out and catch up. As soon as we sat down he began regaling me with requests for networking tips for his new business endeavor. Be transparent on the premise of your get-togethers. I felt misled on the purpose of our evening.

A few months later, I attended a neighborhood party. I'd been traveling a lot and was looking forward to catching up with friends. Upon arrival I was waylaid by an acquaintance grilling me on tips for a conference she was running in a couple of weeks. My opportunity to unwind morphed into an exhausting energy drain.

If you want to pick my brain, say it outright. I'm happy to help. What I don't like is being backed into talking shop at a chill gathering. Even we introverts appreciate casual socializing at times. What we don't like is being caught off guard. Or being cornered by people who mysteriously reach out only when they need something. Don't harsh my mellow. This is a terrible foundation for any kind of networking.

Notes from the Field
"Don't Ask!"

I was recently temporarily confined to getting around on crutches. Besides discovering new dimensions of my propensity for clumsiness (steer clear!), I gained further insight into the Introvert Experience.

Just as questions that seem innocuous in a business setting are off-putting to some, the same holds in social settings. A pervasive, seemingly kneejerk, reaction to seeing an acquaintance with a newly minted ailment is to cry out, "What happened?!" The cumulative result of this query is that respondents find themselves in a conversation loop, endlessly recounting the same series of events. Not to mention, the backstory may be personal, depressing, or embarrassing.

People have wildly disparate perceptions of what's private. Asking general questions such as "How ya doing?" lets others take the lead on whether to bring up an observably altered state. Near the end of my convalescence I attended a meeting with four professional women. None initiated a conversation about my condition, letting me, a person they had just met, decide whether to mention it. I was impressed.

Back to you. Following is a three-step system for pursuing new connections. A cool feature of this approach is that many pursuits are free, and most others are low cost.

 Percolate

Ready to apply networking in a social context? Time to mobilize.

PHASE ONE: STEPPING OUT

Start with simple, achievable steps. Explore your surroundings. Discover what's in your neighborhood, or take public transit into town. Be on the lookout for walking trails, farmers markets, gardens, exercise loops, shared public spaces, or even dog parks (if you, ah, have a dog).

Peruse websites, local newsletters, and bulletin boards. Ask around. Pop into stores and civic buildings to learn about upcoming events. I polled folks settling into new locations and/or embarking on fresh beginnings. Here are some of their tips:

- If possible, choose a place to live with easy access to local activities.
- Head to a neighborhood café to work or research the area. You're being productive while putting yourself in a position to potentially meet others.
- Be extra friendly to cashiers, baristas, waitstaff, bartenders, and shopkeepers. You'll soon feel more at home in frequented establishments.
- Explore online resources for organized meetups. You'll discover endless genres featuring a slew of events.
- Say yes! When on the fence, opt to try something new.
- Rideshare to work. Meet new people, save money, drive less, conserve resources.
- Host a BBQ, housewarming, potluck, or game night, inviting folks you've met.
- If you're frustrated by slow progress, give yourself a break. Take time off to regroup. Keep your expectations in check.

PHASE TWO: SIGN UP

The next step is attending structured programs. This has three distinct benefits:

- You engage in an activity or topic you enjoy.
- You have an interest in common with others attending.
- You gain skills, acquire knowledge, and learn something new.

Head to the event with the intention of enjoying the program. Acquiring a new BFF is not required to make your time worthwhile. Options fall into three general categories:

Events

- Alumni programs (schools, past affiliations, camps, scouting)
- Lectures (topics, genres, and speakers of all ilks)
- Museums (tours, after-hour events, docent training)

Classes

- Continuing professional education
- Degree and certificate-based programs
- Interests (architecture, crafts, food and wine, and the like)

Clubs and Special Interest Groups

- Professional societies
- Book and film clubs
- Sports and interest leagues (bowling, soccer, chess)

Be on the lookout for volunteer opportunities. You can collaborate with a team (shelters and food banks), obtain free access to events (theater ushers), and gain useful skills (recording books for the sight-impaired). Making a real difference in others' lives (senior homes, literacy programs, crisis hotlines) enhances your own. Lift your spirits while expanding your reach beyond your daily sphere.

When you need to get away, consider thematic retreats or organized group vacations. Increasing in popularity, options are cropping up like dandelions these days.

Pace

Modern living typically plays out in the two primary venues of home and work. We go back and forth between the two. Each brings a share of demands and responsibilities. Yet there are also *third places* with an appeal all their own.

Background

As the Industrial Revolution made homes more self-sufficient, leisure activities shifted away from public gathering places. Families began to spend a higher percentage of time within their private dwellings.

The trend persists. Until a few decades ago, enjoying movies and video games meant heading out to the cinema or arcade. Now most forms of entertainment can take place in the comfort of one's living room. On top of this, the proliferation of the internet means we can even do many errands without leaving home. With a reduced impetus to venture out, we are increasingly siloed into individual worlds.

What's more, virtual workspaces, telecommuting, and home offices are fusing the standard two places into one. While these options offer convenience and benefits, they can also lead to physical and mental isolation. As these collective trends expand, with no reversal in sight, the need for a third place is increasingly urgent. The concept has been popularized by Ray Oldenburg's *The Great Good Place*, among other works.

Discovering Your Third Place

The third place, also called a third space, can be traced to the Asian teahouse. Unlike fast-food establishments, where speed is of the essence, the teahouse invites patrons to linger. The message conveyed is to relax and enjoy yourself.

In a third place you can unwind from daily stressors, free from the pressures of work and home. These are informal meeting places, with specifics varying by location. In the U.K. the corner pub epitomizes the third place of choice.

Third places are community anchors, fostering broader interactions than those offered in standard workplaces. Characteristics include easy accessibility, the unimportance of social status, and openness to regulars and newcomers alike. Examples include:

- Community center (i.e. YMCA)
- Neighborhood café
- Gym or fitness center
- Tabletop gaming store
- Library or bookshop
- Place of worship

Despite diverse backdrops, a well-appointed third place offers warmth, rejuvenation, and a sense of belonging. The TV sitcom *Cheers* (1982–1993) was one of the most popular series of all time. Episodes centered on interactions among regulars at a neighborhood bar. The theme song, "Where Everybody Knows Your Name," captured the show's essence. The sense of belonging conveyed in the storylines had enormous appeal.

Take Action!
"A Place to Call Your Own"

Test-drive third-place options that complement your lifestyle. Expand your horizons and consider out-of-the-box possibilities as well. Find one with potential? Visit several times, aiming to arrive consistently around the same time. A third place for many is a gym or workout facility. However, the makeup of these communities fluctuates based on the time of day, with an entirely different vibe in the morning and at night.

Discovering a home away from home can rebalance—even transform—daily living.

Notes from the Field

Honk If You Love Honking!

You're in a hurry; I get it. We've all got places to go. I'm as busy as the next writer, deciding where to place my commas.

Particularly if you live in a major metropolitan area, there's an outside chance you spend an exasperating percentage of time behind the wheel. Traffic makes you late and irate! (That's a pretty good one, admit it.) You are certain that the jerk merging late was trying to cut you off, not merely lost and confused. Plus, the slowpoke ahead is cruising an intolerable 12 mph below the speed limit.

HONK! HONK-HONK!!!

I admit I've been known to honk once or twice a year. My kids claim it's closer to once a day, but who's counting? All this is to say, I feel your pain. Yet ponder this: are you more polite and patient face-to-face than with anonymous drivers on the street? If so, how about transferring some of that "real you" to the driver's seat? Giving people the benefit of the doubt, waving others ahead of you, permitting a less-than-legal merge, relaxing into the traffic situation at hand, is good for your blood pressure and karma.

When I lived in the small town of Ithaca, New York, people were very friendly in their driving habits, due in no small part to the high likelihood that drivers would know each other personally. Try pretending the same is true where you reside.

The fact is, you never know who is driving next to you. Could be a current or pending connection. In a memorable example (I swear this time it wasn't me!) an unnamed person was racing to get to a job interview. She was stuck winding around in a busy parking garage at the last minute. Held up by a car slowly backing into a space ahead, she honked impatiently and cruised past. She received a glare from the driver—who turned out to be her interviewer. 'Nuff said.

Related Sundry Tips

Free will. The beauty of social networking is that free will reigns. You call the shots, attending only events you deem worthy of your time. If someone rubs you the wrong way, you don't have to be on a project team with him for the next two years.

Reserve judgment. A colleague, Maria, recounted a story of her superficial contact with an acquaintance, Gloria. Maria considered Gloria irritating, though she couldn't pinpoint why. One day Maria went to a blood drive where Gloria was volunteering. Caring and empathetic, Gloria tended to Maria's donation. Maria opened up to her about a medical condition. Now, Maria can't say enough good things about Gloria, a cherished friend. Maria learned a hefty lesson about groundless judgments.

Be chill. There's no reason to get all worked up. Being chill is appealing. Flying off the handle? Not so much. A cooking school instructor shared a story of students coming to blows over a dispute regarding stirring techniques. Only her physical intervention halted the fist fight. Turns out, even petite chefs pack a punch. Must be all that kneading.

Illustrations abound. I attended a fabulous teambuilding program involving simulated space travel. This exemplary training did a bang-up job of conveying a sense of realism. My designated copilot took the simulation so seriously that he shouted at me incessantly, concerned that time would run out before we could rescue our imagined comrade on a spacewalk. My response—nervous laughter—just fueled the fire. Maintain perspective.

Be reliable. Some themes resonate in social *and* business networking. Being reliable demonstrates you've got your act together. Be positive, the kind of person you'd want to hang around. Show up on time. Seek out opportunities to do good. Honor your word. To ensure you make only promises you can keep, think twice before making commitments.

Streamline. Even extroverts benefit from resisting the urge to jump on the bandwagon of every sign-up sheet crossing their path. Test the waters of up to three options at a time.

Cut slack. Not everyone is looking to make new friends. Introverts find it stressful to have too many obligations. Extroverts may extend an offer to hang out yet not follow through. Someone brushes past you? Turns down an invitation? Doesn't follow up? Resist the inclination to take it personally. An excellent mantra: "It's not about me." Chin up!

Hitting the refresh button on life gobbles up a lot of energy. Can't remember the last time you sat down to a stimulating conversation deconstructing a favorite movie with a good buddy? Visit an old friend. A change of scenery and some good laughs might be precisely what the doctor ordered.

see ya later, alligator

Carefully observe the way your heart draws you; and choose

that way with all your strength.

—Hasidic proverb

Are You STILL Here? Quiz

Select the proper response(s). Now that you have stuck around to the end, you:

a. Are a bit older and wiser than when you began.

b. Have learned the secret chant to transform introverts into extroverts.

c. Can leverage your innate strengths to jump-start a networking journey.

a + c

Your Inner Field Guide

When do you light up? When do you fade back? Follow your gut. If advice rings true, a light bulb will illuminate over your head. If not, let it go.

Connectivity is the new, improved way to build a strong, lasting network.

Put your best self out there. Pretending to be someone you're not is so 2008.

UPON REFLECTION

I don't believe we learn from experience. I can do the same foolishness repeatedly without getting a whit wiser. Learning evolves from *reflecting on* experience. Recognizing patterns and extracting lessons is how we develop and deepen. Consider the following presupposition, a basic precept of NLP (introduced in chapter 8):

There is no such thing as failure, only feedback.

Thinking *I failed* is a copout! You're so not off the hook; I run a tight ship.

Try this on for size. Reframe setbacks as opportunities for change and signals for continual improvement. This approach requires more responsibility than *I blew it*. Explode your limiting mindset.

What would happen if you replaced the concept of failure with that of opportunity?

This is the Chinese character for crisis. It is composed of two stacked figures. Wēi, danger, is above and jī, opportunity, is below. As the complete character implies, what initially appears as danger is a cover for opportunity.

Take Action!
"The Point of It All"

You can exceed your perceived boundaries, in networking and beyond. I'm here to prove it, and we've no time to lose.

Get off that couch. Stand up, get your blood flowing. Hold nothing. Put one arm straight ahead, index finger pointing directly in front of you. Next, reach that arm as far back behind you as possible, while keeping the rest of your body still facing forward. Now peek back and see how far back you stretched your arm, turning your head around to look without shifting your arm. Notice what you are pointing to behind you.

Shake out. Assume the identical starting location and repeat the exercise, and *this time reach farther*. Peek again. Did you point farther? Remarkably, every person among the myriad I have engaged in this activity has reached farther the second time. What was the difference between the first time and the second? One tiny detail: the imperative to go farther. Even though the first time I said to reach as far back as possible. This shift in outcome makes no sense! If you were following the instructions, you reached as far as you could the first time! How is it possible to reach even farther only a moment later? You tell me.

Appendix

CHEAT SHEET!

Introverts	Extroverts
Think to talk	Talk to think
Seek depth	Seek breadth
Energize alone	Energize with others
Reflective	Verbal
Focused	Expansive
Self-reliant	Social
Value Privacy	Value Sharing

Focus

Introverts	Extroverts
Inner-Directed	Outer-Directed
Thoughts & Ideas	People & Events
Need Concentration	Need Diversions

Networking Preferences

Introverts	Extroverts
Listening	Speaking
Few stimuli	High stimuli
One-on-one	Groups

Networking Strategies

Introverts	Extroverts
1. Prep (Research)	1. Patter (Discuss)
2. Percolate (Connect)	2. Promote (Sell)
3. Pace (Restore)	3. Party (Socialize)

Relevant Reads

Bandler, Richard, and John Grinder. *Reframing: Neuro-Linguistic Programming and the Transformation of Meaning*. Salt Lake City, UT: Real People Press, 1982.

Bengtsson, Ingemar, and Karol Zyczkowski. *Geometry of Quantum States: Second Edition*. Cambridge: Cambridge University Press, 2017.

Biech, Elaine, ed. *Trainers Warehouse Book of Games: Fun and Energizing Ways to Enhance Learning*. San Francisco: Pfeiffer, 2008.

Buber, Martin. *I and Thou*. New York, NY: Touchstone, 1971.

Fischer, Roger, & Ury, William. *Getting to Yes*, 2nd ed. New York, NY: Penguin, 2011.

Frankl, Victor. *Man's Search for Meaning*. New York, NY: Beacon Press, 2006.

Gladwell, Malcolm. *Blink*. New York, NY: Little, Brown, 2007.

Gladwell, Malcolm. *David and Goliath*. New York, NY: Back Bay Books, 2015.

Hoff, Benjamin. *The Tao of Pooh*. New York, NY: Penguin 1983.

Howard, Pierce. *The Owner's Manual for the Brain*, 4th ed. New York, NY: William Morrow, 2014.

Kador, John. *301 Best Questions to Ask on Your Interview*. New York, NY: McGraw-Hill, 2010.

Kahnweiler, Jennifer. *The Introverted Leader*, 2nd ed. Oakland, CA: Berrett-Koehler, 2018.

Kroeger, Otto, and Janet Thuesen. *Type Talk at Work*, 2nd ed. New York, NY: Delta, 2002.

Matei, Sorin, and Brian Britt. *Structural Differentiation in Social Media*. Berlin, Germany: Springer, 2017.

Myers, Isabel B., Mary H. McCaulley, Naomi L. Quenk, and Allen L. Hammer. *Myers-Briggs Type Indicator Manual*. Saint Paul, MN: Consulting Psychologist Press, 1998.

Oldenburg, Ray. *The Great Good Place*, 3rd ed. New York, NY: Marlowe & Co., 1999.

Zack, Devora. *Managing for People Who Hate Managing*. San Francisco: Berrett-Koehler, 2012.

Zack, Devora. *Singletasking*. San Francisco: Berrett-Koehler, 2015.

Acknowledgments

Thank you Jeevan Sivasubramaniam. I used to wonder how authors got so lucky as to thank their "publisher and friend," and now it is my turn. Jeevan also happens to be my illustrator, confidant, nemesis, and alter ego. This book would not exist without him. I also kvell over my editor, Neal Maillet; his heart of gold embodies compassion and kindness. Together, they're huge mensches . . . and highly entertaining.

Heartfelt appreciation goes out to the entire, inimitable BK team for your spectacular support year after year. My life and books are richer for knowing and collaborating with you. Thanks for persistently imploring me to write a second edition. Like any self-respecting introvert, I hid out as long as possible before joining the crusade.

Thank you, James Killian, my high school English teacher, for teaching me how to write and, parenthetically, how to live.

A million hugs to my three unbelievable teenage sons for everything you are and do. Gratitude also goes out to my widespread friends and family for your boundless support. If I mentioned each of you by name, my entire platform as an introvert would again be called into question.

Last, and the opposite of least, I thank Evan, who saves the day again and again, all while affirming how much he believes in me.

index

communities for networkers
asking personal questions, 162
attending structured programs, 163–164
background, 165
being chill, 168
being reliable, 168–169
classes, 164
clubs, 164
cutting slack, 169
differentiating, 161
events, 164
exploring your surroundings, 162–163
free will, 168
pacing, 160–162, 165
percolating, 162–164
pursuing new connections, 162
reserving judgment, 168
special interest groups, 164
streamlining, 169
third places, 166–167
unwinding, 165
connectivity. *See* interconnectivity.
context for goals, 98–99
control for goals, 98–99
conversation management at networking
events, 83–84
conversations
ending, 80–81, 123
sparking, 92, 122–123, 124–128
crisis, Chinese character for, 172
cutting slack, 169

D

deep breathing, 35
definition, 16
demographics of generational variances,
58–59
departure plan from networking events,
80–81
differentiating, 161
DJ on college radio, 93
doing your part, 139–140
dressing for networking events, 76
drinking adult beverages at networking
events, 79
driving habits of introverts, 167
Dunbar's number, 32

E

e-mail
guidelines, 45
preference for, 121

eating alone, 62
ecology for goals, 98, 100
Einstein, Albert, 19
elasticity, 12–13
elevator pitch, 107
employment. *See* job search.
ending conversations, 80–81, 123
engaging out of type, 52–53
events for networking. *See* networking
events.
expansiveness among extroverts, 30
exploring your surroundings, 162–163
Extroland, 22–24
extroversion, pros and cons, 3
extroverts
expansiveness, 30
in the general population, 3
identifying, 22–24, 28–29
integrating with introverts and
centroverts, 136
interpreting events and exchanges, 50
labels, 24
online platforms for interconnectivity,
31–32
percolating, 90
a perfect day, 91
principles, 72
reenergizing, 30–31
socializing, 30–31
stereotypes, 23
teamwork, 29
verbal expression, 30
vs. introverts. *See* introverts *vs.*
extroverts.
eye contact at networking events, 77

F

failure *vs.* feedback, 172
faxes, as networking resource, 94–96
fight-or-flight response, 34–35
first impressions, 105–106
flexibility. *See* mental elasticity.
flexing your style, 52–53, 56
focus
among introverts, 26–27
characteristic of introversion, 10
on others at networking events, 79
on yourself at networking events, 80
follow-up communication
being useful, 152
excessive, 153–154
failure, flimsy excuses for, 146–148

generational variances, 58
letting go, 156–157
outside the box, 155
pacing yourself, 154–155
percolating, 151–153
personalizing, 152
prepping for, 149
resilience, 149–150
squeaky wheels, 153–154
submissions, 152–153
timing, 151
waiting for response, 153
food stations at networking events, 78
frat parties, 93
free will, 168

G

Generation X, generational variances, 58–59
generational variances
baby boomers, 58–59
business cards, 58
demographics, 58–59
follow-up communication, 58
Generation X, 58–59
iGens, 58–59
meeting attire, 58
message styles, 58
Millennial, 58–59
office behavior, 59
phones *vs.* cell phones, 59
weekends and holidays, 59
Gladwell, Malcolm, 104
goals, at networking events, 76, 96–98
goals, elements of positive outcomes
context, 98–99
control, 98–99
ecology, 98, 100
measurability, 98, 100
positive statements, 97, 99
template for, 99–100
golden rule *vs.* platinum rule, 48–52
graduate school interviews, 115
The Great Good Place, 166

H

hating networking
catastrophic thinking, 38
deep breathing, 35
failure of ordinary advice, 36–38
fight-or-flight response, 34–35

inner monologues, 38
promotions, 40
reframing, 39–40
relaxation response, 35
saber-toothed tigers, 34–35
self-image, 42–43
self-talk, 40–41, 44
high-frequency questions at networking events, 83–84

I

I/E (introversion/extroversion) continuum. *See also* introverts *vs.* extroverts.
centroverts, 16
clear preferences, 16
definition, 16
innate preferences, 18
slight preferences, 19
strength of preference, 16–20
strong preferences, 16, 19
typing out, 16
identifying
centroverts, 22–24
extroverts, 22–24, 28–29, 174
introverts, 22–24, 24–25, 174
iGens, generational variances, 58–59
information table at networking events, 77
informational interviews, 113–114
innate preferences, 18
inner-direction, among introverts, 27–28
inner monologues, 38
instant messaging, as networking resource, 94–96, 121
interconnectivity
building networks, 172
definition, 19–20
Dunbar's number, 32
maximum capacity for social networks, 32
online platforms for, 31–32
super-connectors, 31–32
interpreting events and exchanges, 50
interruptions, introverts dealing with, 27
interviewing for a job. *See* job search, interview tips.
introducing yourself, 107–110
introversion, pros and cons, 28
introversion/extroversion (I/E) continuum. *See* I/E (introversion/extroversion) continuum.

About Only Connect Consulting

Only Connect Consulting, Inc. (OCC) is an award-winning international leadership development firm with over 100 clients in every major sector. Since 1996, OCC has grown annually as an entirely referral-based business.

SAMPLE CLIENTS

Smithsonian, Deloitte, Mensa, U.S. Department of Education, Delta Airlines, Global Intellectual Properties Academy, McGraw-Hill UK, Environmental Protection Agency, Urban Land Institute, John Deere, and U.S. Patent and Trademark Office.

Ms. Zack, CEO, has also taught at Johns Hopkins Medical Institute, London School of Business, Cornell University, National Institute of Health, University of Pittsburgh, Treasury Executive Institute, Ohio State, University of Maryland, American Management Association, the Australian Institute of Management, and a slew more, albeit we're in danger of extending past the page count allowance.

OCC won the USDA Woman-Owned Business of the Year award.

AREAS OF EXPERTISE

- Leadership Development
- Singletasking
- Change Management
- Presentation Skills
- Time/Stress Management
- Creative Problem Solving
- Organizational Assessments

- Networking
- Team Development
- Communication
- Customer Service
- 360-Degree Feedback
- Coaching/Mentoring
- Meeting Facilitation

- Myers-Briggs Type Indicator
- Managing Up
- Conflict Management
- Theater-Based Simulations

- Strategic Planning
- Productivity
- Influence/Negotiation
- Focus Groups

Featured Media

OCC and Ms. Zack have been featured in dozens of worldwide media such as the *Wall Street Journal, USA Today, ABC-TV, Time, US News & World Report, CNN Money, CNBC, Fox Business-TV, British Airways, Forbes, Cosmo, Self, Redbook, Women's Health, Working Mother, Globe and Mail, Fast Company,* and many publications in languages she cannot, let's be honest, read without a translator.

For additional information and bookings, visit www.myonlyconnect.com.

 Your Fearless Author

Our greatest glory is not in never failing but in rising each time we fail.

—Confucius

A resident of Introville, Devora commutes to Extroland for work. After a productive childhood of reading stacks of books and playing games by herself, she received a BA, magna cum laude, from University of Pennsylvania. Putting her degree to good use, she proceeded to freelance as an actress, disc jockey in the United States and Italy, London chambermaid, tap dancer, hotline counselor, and investigative reporter. In each of these endeavors, she strove to keep conversation to a minimum.

After passing Go, she collected an MBA from Cornell University (Johnson Graduate School of Management), where she was a full-tuition merit scholar.

Devora is interested in the nuances of personality, food, and stuff that sparkles. She founded Only Connect Consulting, Inc. (OCC) in 1996 and is pleased to have been hired by innumerable top-notch, overwhelmed, underconnected clients.

She is a *Washington Post* best-selling author, keynote speaker, consultant, and coach. Her books, *Singletasking* (Berrett-Koehler, 2015), *Managing for People Who Hate Managing* (Berrett-Koehler, 2012), and

Networking for People Who Hate Networking (Berrett-Koehler, 2010) are in forty-five language editions.

Devora served as visiting faculty at Cornell University's MBA Leadership Skills Program for fifteen years. She keynotes and lectures around the world for corporations, universities, federal agencies, non-profits, associations, law firms, and, well, you get the idea. She teaches networking, singletasking, leadership, presentation skills, communication, change management, and teamwork—then retreats to dine alone.

Her revolutionary new approaches to professional and personal development emphasize self-knowledge, acceptance of differences, and authenticity. Awards include Top Ten Business Books of 2015, Top Five Business Books of 2016, and Top Ten Non-Fiction by the *Washington Post*.

Devora is a certified practitioner in neuro-linguistic programming and the Myers-Briggs Type Indicator. She is also a member of Phi Beta Kappa and Mensa.

And that's a wrap.

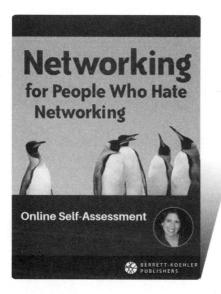

The *GET TO IT!* Toolkit

Enroll in the official *Networking for People Who Hate Networking* Micro-Course!

You've READ it, now LIVE it! Build your networking skills in 3–5 minutes a day on a mobile device or PC.

- Enhance your confidence and knowledge via true-to-life virtual scenarios.
- Put your skills to the test in real-world missions—scored within three workdays.
- Earn free learning experiences for yourself or people you love.
- Try it today risk-free!

Available now on the Talented™ Learning Experience Platform: www.talentedapp.com/bk/networking

Bulk-order discounts available for organizational programs.

Berrett–Koehler Publishers, Inc.
www.bkconnection.com

Dear reader,

Thank you for picking up this book and welcome to the worldwide BK community! You're joining a special group of people who have come together to create positive change in their lives, organizations, and communities.

What's BK all about?

Our mission is to connect people and ideas to create a world that works for all.

Why? Our communities, organizations, and lives get bogged down by old paradigms of self-interest, exclusion, hierarchy, and privilege. But we believe that can change. That's why we seek the leading experts on these challenges—and share their actionable ideas with you.

A welcome gift

To help you get started, we'd like to offer you a **free copy** of one of our bestselling ebooks:

www.bkconnection.com/welcome

When you claim your **free ebook**, you'll also be subscribed to our blog.

Our freshest insights

Access the best new tools and ideas for leaders at all levels on our blog at ideas.bkconnection.com.

Sincerely,

Your friends at Berrett-Koehler